My Way

My Way

A Memoir

Dear Father:
Much good
luck and best
wishes to you
and yours —
Jessie
July 2015

Jessie Halkias

ISBN-13: 978-1943324019

ISBN-10: 1943324018

Library of Congress Control Number: 2014960168

BISAC Category:

Biography and Autobiography/Personal Memoirs

Names of some individuals mentioned in this story, who are not members of the family, have been changed to protect their privacy.

All quotes from the *Rubáiyát* of Omar Khayám are taken from the translation by Edward Fitzgerald, 1933 Edition

Third Printing, 2015

Story Preserves, LLC

Denver, Colorado 80222

www.storypreserves.com

Storypreserves@gmail.com

Dedicated to my son John,
who walked his entire life in the shadow
of his father,
and to my daughters, Penny, Stephanie and Katherine.
This is my gift to you.

Acknowledgements

No matter how far you go remember where you're from.

Anonymous

Without the encouragement of Phyllis and Roger Beatty, Beth Coyle, Yvonne Rodler, and Khalil Dabaghi, I would never have attempted to write this book, and without the perseverance and guidance provided by my publisher Angela Keane, I never would have finished it.

Some of the events of my life were bitter, unpleasant, or just plain sad; but it felt necessary to include them, because along with the good times—and there were oh so many!—all of these events contributed to my story.

None of what I have written was meant to offend or harm anyone, and it is my fervent hope that it is received in the spirit of which it is written.

My gratitude extends to all the many friends that I have known and loved along the way, and who made contributions to molding me into who I am. You are the potters, I am the clay.

I extend my deepest love to my daughters, Penny, Stephanie and Katherine for their dedication, love and support.

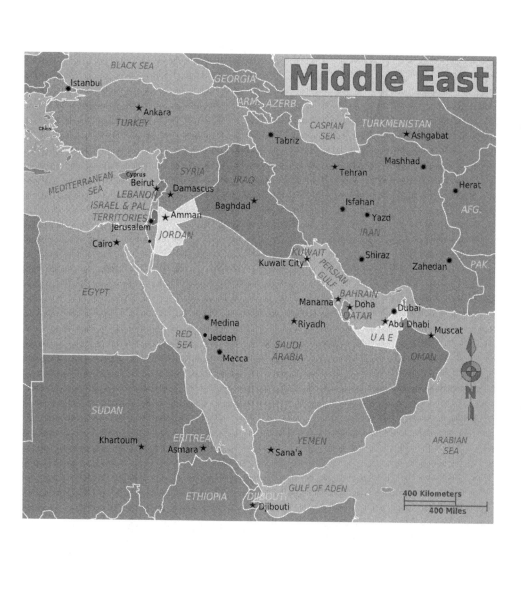

I have only told the half of what I saw.

Marco Polo

Looking back over my life, I have always been a dreamer. As a child, I dreamed of visiting Mesopotamia and ended up seeing the world, well, a large part of it anyway. After high school, my dream was to attend college in Galesburg, Illinois. Instead, the Middle East became the center of my life for more than 50 years.

It frightened my mother when I flew off to Iraq to work at the American Embassy, then married a man, who was highly thought of and respected both in the business world as well as the social communities, but whom I barely knew. Ever ready for adventure, I was rewarded beyond my dreams.

My journey has been amazing thus far, but not exempt from suffering. Painful events in my life have brought me to my knees, yet I remain in awe of the wonders of this world, and my life has been rich with love and abundance. Writing this book has been, if not the most, one of the most emotional experiences of my life.

Some of the most memorable sights I have had the privilege to behold are the plunge of Niagara Falls; driving east across the Saudi Arabian Peninsula from Jeddah on the Red Sea to Dammam on the Arabian Gulf; flying from Teheran to Kabul in a small plane weaving its way in and out through the mountains; driving across Kansas in May and seeing the hundreds of acres of wheat waving in the breeze. And so much more.

Like Marco Polo, on the pages that follow, I give you only half of what I've seen—so far.

Contents

Part I

Life is a great big canvas, and you should throw all the paint on it you can.

Danny Kaye

Kentucky

Growing up during the depression years in Western Kentucky, my childhood was plain and simple. My father, Arley Rudolph, was a tradesman who worked from home in his shop on our property. He fashioned things, almost anything, from metal. He was musical, with knowledge of the guitar, mandolin, piano, and best of all, the violin. Daddy was also a beekeeper or apiarist and kept as many as fifty hives. These little creatures were fascinating to me as a child. As well, he was a taxidermist—and had beautiful handwriting. With little formal education, most of Daddy's knowledge was self-taught. When he came upon a subject (any subject) which interested him, he would send a written order for "how to" instructions.

Our mother took care of my brother Morris and me. Mother had a spirit that wouldn't quit, along with a colorful way of expressing herself. I expect many of her sayings came from her Irish/Chickasaw mother. There were just the two of us children, and I was the younger by one year.

When we made a trip to Paducah, a town of about 40,000, this was a big event. We usually went *to town*, as we called it, on Saturdays. There were neighborhood kids close by where we lived; together in the summertime, we roamed the fields and woods, waded in the creek, and in general tormented most of our neighbors. In those days no one locked their doors. Once, with one of my playmates, we walked into a neighbor's kitchen, found a fresh pie in the pantry and simply helped ourselves to half of it. Needless to say, later we were solidly reprimanded.

Daddy never worked the fields; the 80 acres of farmland we owned were leased out. However, we did have a workhorse named Clipper. Sometimes I was allowed to ride Clipper—in the fields of course. Someone else raised the tobacco and corn crops on a simple two-thirds, one-third lease. We had a little orchard, and Daddy had his vegetable garden. There were all manner of vegetables growing. In late summer, when the weather became cooler and the growing season was over, a vegetable hill was prepared in one corner of the garden. It was a large mound of dirt lined with straw. There we stored cabbages, carrots and turnips that were eaten throughout the fall. The contents of the hill were very useful and lasted well into the winter. Ah, the halcyon days of childhood.

These were the 1930s, the depression years. Not everybody, but almost everyone, was poor. Our main objective was getting through the winter and having or finding the money to pay the real estate taxes. Not income taxes—there was no such thing in those days. Glory be!

A large part of my summers was spent at the home of Uncle Ollie Holt, Mother's younger brother, and his wife, Aunt Viola. Even though their home was about 18 miles away from us, they were almost my second parents and of course were very special to me. Nancy, my aunt's youngest sister, lived with them. We were close in age and best friends. As my mother would say, "What one of you couldn't think of to do, the other would."

A good part of our time was spent sliding down dirt banks, agitating the neighbor's bull, then finding out which one of us would get out of his path the soonest and back over the fence. Climbing up into the rafters of the barn, we found the sparrows' nests and robbed the eggs. We fished in the pond, collected tadpoles in jars, and kept them until they died. Fireflies at nightfall were also put in jars until of course they too died.

For a quick snack, we climbed up the wild grape vines to pick the sour grapes. When no one was looking, we took the vines, which had to be exactly the right size and length; corn silk; rabbit tobacco, a wild plant considered by some as medicinal for colds and flu, and even oats, and used them as *tobacco*. We papered them with newspaper and smoked away. At that time, not one of us knew a thing about global warming, over-population, smog, let alone the hazards of smoking on our health.

Some of the neighborhood boys had learned that tin foil, collected from cigarette packs, candy wrappers and what not, could be sold. So one of the summertime pastimes was collecting the foil and wrapping it up into a ball. Somehow, somewhere, we did sell it to gain a few extra pennies to buy an all-day sucker or a penny stick of candy.

It was a simpler time, and because people didn't have money, they found other ways to have fun. One of the things the grownups did was *shiveree* the newlyweds in the neighborhood. Late at night, when the couple was in bed, (honeymoons were a rarity) all the neighbors walked over to their home and banged on pots and pans to wake them up. As children, we weren't included in this ritual, but we all heard about it the next day.

There were also *play parties* on a regular basis. A group of neighbors, referred to as *regulars*, would gather on a weekend evening. Any one talented enough, whether it be on the piano, violin, mandolin, or guitar would play the music and everyone would dance.

I have always loved coconut, especially as a child. In some respects it was a rarity in our lives. However, about once a month, my mother would make a coconut cake or two (always two) coconut pies. She would press a dime in my hand and send me off to the neighborhood grocery store to buy coconut. I was to exchange the ten cents for the coconut which was put into a small brown bag to take back to Mother. What a difficult task it was to walk the 300 yards back home without sampling the coconut! Usually I made it back with tasting only some (well, not much anyway) of the brown bag contents. One particular time I didn't make it and ended up eating well over half of the bag's worth. When I realized what I'd done, I was afraid to go home and face Mother. However, I did and received the tongue lashing of my life along with a sound spanking. I was returned to the store with another dime, this time to bring the full dime's worth of coconut home to Mother and did so.

Uncle Ollie, being a farmer, kept cows. He taught me to milk the cows, so of course Nancy and I helped with the milking each morning and evening. We also learned to *sucker* tobacco. The tobacco-growing season lasted from May to August. Small shoots would appear between the leaves of the tobacco plant, and these shoots had be removed two or three times during the growing season; otherwise, they would sap the strength of the plant. Women and neighbors helped with this chore. We would walk up and down the rows pushing the suckers out. Our hands became black and sticky. Nancy and I probably lasted a half hour or so at most, but we liked doing it and believed we were helping.

The month of August was canning season, and Mother canned peaches, green beans, corn and sauerkraut in fruit jars. My job was to wash the glass jars as they were re-used from year to year. We only replaced the lids with fresh new ones equipped with sealer rubber bands.

Nancy and I loved sleeping on a pallet on the floor, giggling and punching each other until we fell asleep. When my aunt and uncle would leave us alone at home with her grandmother, Mammy Sir, we'd often play on the telephone. The phone was a large contraption that hung high on the wall, and we needed to climb onto a chair to properly operate this piece of equipment. In those days, we had what was called *party lines* where the same phone line was shared with a number of households, each one having a different ring. It was easy to listen in on the neighbors' conversations; it was how we kept up on what was going on in the neighborhood!

To reach your party it was necessary to ring the phone with a crank-like ringer a certain number of times, be they long or short rings. We might call a number, any number, and when someone answered, "Hello," we would say, "We want to speak to Gene Autry." We did this often enough that the phone operator called my uncle to complain. She told him to keep us off the phone. We were so embarrassed and ashamed when we were found out; we wanted to wither up and die. But, as I recall, we never got into any real trouble.

Uncle Ollie and Aunt Viola were very religious, and they attended church every Sunday morning as well as prayer meetin' night on Wednesday evenings. On Sundays, when I stayed with them, Nancy and I had our baths in the washtub, sometimes in the same water, got dressed in our Sunday best (which wasn't much), put shoes on, and were carried off in the back of the truck to the Bethlehem Baptist Church a few miles outside of Wickliffe, the nearest town. It is at this churchyard cemetery where my husband and son are buried, as well as my parents.

Having lost two or three babies, my aunt and uncle decided in 1943 to adopt a baby boy. They named him James Edward and called him Jimmy. By that time my family had moved to Illinois. Jimmy, however, is the closest relative that remains outside my immediate family. Two or three times a year, I visit Kentucky and always enjoy seeing Jimmy and his wife, Diann.

Uncle Ollie lived to be 90. This man would give you the shirt off his back whether you needed it or not. Uncle Ollie developed stomach cancer, but that's not how he died. He had gone to church on Sunday morning and was told there was something wrong with the church furnace. Viola was still alive at the time but had developed dementia and lived in a nursing home. He came back in the afternoon with some of the men to fix the furnace, but he didn't have the right tools. He told everyone he was going back to get the tools but instead went home and got his gun, returned to the church, parked his truck, and reached into the seat of the truck and said, "Hey, all of you, look here." He put the gun to his mouth and shot himself in front of all of them. I don't know if he had brought the tools back or not; I got this story from Diann. She phoned me in Egypt with the news. It is shocking to remember how he died.

Mother had a younger brother, Uncle Elton, who died in 1946, after we had moved to Illinois. He died in a stupid accident. Uncle Elton drank heavily. Going down the country road, he overturned his tractor and landed in a ditch. He lay for a number of hours in the water. He wasn't dead when they found him, but he died shortly thereafter. His wife, Lucile, had long, stringy hair which she seldom washed, but we had great fun together. Sometimes when I'd go to their house, we'd sit on the floor and play jacks. We had the best time. I really liked her but am not sure what the rest of our family thought about her.

My father's marriage to my mother was his second marriage. His first wife Thelma died of tuberculosis after two and a half years; there were no children. Mother was 18 years old and very pretty; Daddy was 32 when they eloped. Daddy, a good looking man, was a correct gentleman in all respects, having been brought up by a strong mother who tolerated no nonsense. Ma Rudolph, as we called our grandmother, was a most religious person. She was a Pentecostal Christian, or in those days what some people referred to as *holy rollers*. My grandfather was content to sit back and let grandmother run the show. As I remember him, he was a bit of a lump.

Morris and I were the only grandchildren. My father's younger brother Davis was abnormal, no doubt injured at birth or born with a congenital birth defect. He never married but was a kind, gentle, dear man who loved my brother and me very much. Unfortunately, the neighbor children labeled him the *village idiot* and delighted in throwing rocks at him and taunting him in a general manner just to get a reaction out of him. My father also had a sister who died as a newborn. My grandparents never talked about her. It was my mother who told me she had been the third child of my grandparents.

I remember clearly a warm spring day in 1940. Mother and Daddy had left me home alone while they took a trip to town. When they were in Paducah, a stranger in a car stopped at our house. She was carrying a book and note pad. After announcing her identity, she asked me if I could supply her some information about our family. I was already aware of the up and coming census taking, so of course I was more than happy and proud to do so, all on my own! With my help she recorded the details of our family for the 1940 U.S. Census. I was ten years old at the time.

On an ordinary morning in November of that same year, my brother and I said goodbye to our parents and left for school. When we returned home that afternoon, our father was dead. He had suffered a stroke during the morning and died a few hours later. He was 48 years old.

We were not part of the small group of well-off people in Western Kentucky. As my mother had not finished high school, she was not qualified for skilled labor. She desperately needed work to support us. Mother was very adept at the sewing machine; she was quick and accurate. In her later years, Mother became an avid quilter and quilt maker. She assembled and quilted more than 100 quilts over the span of about 20 years; she created each and every one of them alone. She had no use for the quilting skills of others; their stitches were not fine enough to please her.

Mother owned three incubators, and she hatched and raised her own chickens. One year before Daddy died, she lost 92 baby chickens in the brooder house when rats came in and sucked their blood, leaving the little carcasses. The winter Daddy died, she sold mature chickens as well as eggs to the *rolling store* or *huckster* in exchange for flour and other staples we needed. The rolling store was a large cabinet mounted on the back of a truck that went around the countryside selling groceries and other wares. When stopped, the sides were let down so the shoppers could see what was available. The arrival of the rolling store on its weekly schedule was always an event.

After Daddy died, Mother applied for work at the shirt factory in Paducah. Every day that winter for the next three months, she made her way to the shirt factory to wait outside in the cold with a large group of others in hope of being chosen to begin work. At six o'clock in the morning, she was there waiting for the factory gate to open. Finally in late February 1941, the boss took notice of her there for the umpteenth time, pointed a finger at her, and called out, "You." She was hired on the spot for $2.50 a day. Finally we were in the money!

When I came home from school each day, my chore was to go to the corn crib and chop up the corn which was still on the cob, and feed the chickens. In winter time, I went down to the woods and brought home dead branches which I chopped or broke into pieces that fit into the wood stove. Eventually, when we got a coal stove, I brought in the coal and built a fire so it was ready when Mother returned from work around six in the evening. She was always very tired. More often than not, our evening meal would be bread and milk.

Very shortly after the beginning of World War II, when the Japanese bombed Pearl Harbor on December 7, 1941, our country was put on rationing. The three major items rationed were sugar, coffee and tires. None of this bothered us. Mother had no time to bake sweets, we didn't drink coffee, and we really had no place to go in the old car. These were the days of retread tires, rationing, and Rosie the Riveter.

On May 30, 1942, Mother remarried. David was a good man; he always treated my mother, Morris and me with respect, doing his best to properly provide for us in the way he knew. He was drafted into the U.S. Army and within days of their marriage, he was on his way as a recruit. A year later, on his 38th birthday, he was eligible to apply for discharge and did so. Honorably discharged in July 1943, while our country was still deep into the war, David decided that because factory work was more readily available in Illinois, it would be best to move ourselves there. Morris didn't go with us. He remained in Kentucky with a neighbor family working in their mill for a year before joining us in Pekin where he finished high school. Afterwards he went to work at Alcoa in Bettendorf, Iowa. He married his high school sweetheart, Florence. Florence and I always got along very well. We never had a cross word. She was an only child, and we became like sisters. Actually, I cared almost more for her than I did my brother.

Early in August 1943, on a hot summer morning, Mother, David, and I, in a 1939 Nash (bought with part of David's Army severance pay) loaded to the hilt, set out for Pekin, a town in the Peoria area of central Illinois. There was barely room for me to squeeze in among the few household things in the back seat. David had strapped four spare retreaded tires (only retreads were available) on the roof of the car. By the time we'd traveled 50 miles, we had had five blowouts and were left stranded on the side of the road. In those days there were only two-lane paved highways—when you were lucky.

David left us with the car and walked to the nearest town which was West Frankfurt in Illinois. Within an hour or so he was back with a garage man, and yet another tire. With everything in place, we proceeded into town. By the time the haggling for *good* retreads was over, it was late afternoon. It was decided we would spend the night. The following day we proceeded on to Pekin, our intended destination.

I had recently turned 14 years old.

Illinois

Upon arriving in Pekin, we stayed with relatives for about a week. David applied for work at R. G. LeTourneau in Peoria and was immediately hired. We moved to a rented apartment in Pekin until David and my mother could save enough money to buy a small house. Mother had started work at a shirt factory in Rock Island.

School started shortly after we arrived, and I began my sophomore year at Pekin Community High School. For the next three years we lived within a mile or so of the school. It was normal and natural to walk to and from school. I became comfortable and happy at PCHS, proud to be a member of this student body. I did well in school and graduated in late May of 1946.

Having applied and been accepted at Galesburg College in Galesburg, Illinois, I was filled with dreams. With my classmates, I discussed time and again of going to college, and to me the prospect of Galesburg was no less than grand. My stepfather, however, had different plans for me. With my mother's blessing, David decided I didn't need to spend four years at a college. There was no such thing as student loans in those days. Instead, I should take a course at a two-year business school and learn shorthand, typing, business English, business law, and some accounting. Thus, I would be in a position to support myself after two years instead of spending double that amount of time at Galesburg College. So about a month before graduation, my mother and I paid a visit to Brown's Peoria School of Business. The decision was made.

This was a great disappointment to me. The Monday following high school graduation, I began my classes at Brown's. My mother had learned that because my father had been a World War I veteran, I was eligible to receive educational assistance. As I recall, it was $100 a month. That would be satisfactory. I also learned from the school that I could live with a family in Peoria and do light housekeeping for my room and board, plus be paid $5.00 per week, which I did. So much for Galesburg College.

For 13 months, I lived in Peoria and studied at Brown's. When the educational assistance from the G.I. bill ended after one year, my *higher* education was cut short. It was at school that I met and became good friends with Jean Orahood.

While away at school, Mother and David had moved to East Moline, one of the quad-cities: Moline, Rock Island, East Moline of Illinois and Davenport, Iowa. Upon leaving business school, I also moved to East Moline. It was decided that I could live at home and upon finding a job, would pay $10.00 a week room and board. Hardly more than 18 years old, I was hired at Hickey Brothers in Davenport as one of seven stenographers and became a working girl, earning $125.00 a month. The pay was meager, but our boss, Miss Gremore, was a truly remarkable woman. She was smart, well-educated and a perfectionist. No errors, no misspellings or erasures allowed. She perused each and every letter daily—there were many—and the smallest mistake received a diagonal line in green ink drawn across the entire page. We typed in green ink and our boss, Mr. Hickey, even had a pair of green shoes. The typist who made the mistake was obliged to sit down and retype the entire letter, even if it was after hours. More than once I ended up in tears, but I learned perfection from Miss Gremore.

For one year, I worked for Hickey Brothers, then was eligible for a vacation. As we had decided the previous year, Jean and I made our plans to go to Denver.

Denver

Although I was working in Davenport and Jean was in Chicago, through letters we made travel arrangements for our big two-week vacation. Finally the long awaited day arrived. Jean had a married sister Muff, who lived at 1020 Sherman Street (to be exact), and Jean had arranged with Muff and her husband, Chuck Wifler, to meet us at Union Station in Denver. It was July, 1948.

From Rock Island, I took my first ever train ride to Chicago's Union Station to meet Jean at a predetermined location in the station. Shortly thereafter, we boarded the Rock Island Rocket—in coach of course—for the overnight trip to Denver. Muff and Chuck were waiting to take us to their tiny apartment on Sherman Street. There we were assigned *sleeping quarters* on the fold-out couch in the living room. How imposing can one become!

Muff and Chuck were a dear young couple; they went out of their way to please and make both Jean and me happy. We were given a royal tour of the city as well as the mountains, and then some.

By the end of the first week, Jean and I had decided we wanted to remain in Denver. Staying with Muff and Chuck was too much of an imposition on them; we needed to find another place to live. Perhaps a girls boarding house would be suitable. In searching through the want ads of the newspapers, we found a vacancy at 906 Grant Street, a block from where Muff and Chuck lived. Within hours, we made our visit to Mrs. Curdie's boarding house. Both of us liked what we saw and by the following day had decided to move in, giving Muff and Chuck some peace.

Once the decision was made to remain in Denver, we advised our employers in the Midwest that we were resigning our jobs and would not be returning. We had to find new jobs as quickly as possible, now that we were paying substantial rent. Neither of us had more than a few dollars in our pockets. I found a job at a loan company which I didn't like at all. Also, the pay was poor. So while still working, I kept looking for a better job. Lunch every day was a grilled cheese sandwich and a cup of coffee for 15 cents, plus a penny for tax.

In the newspaper I saw that Stearns-Rogers, an oil equipment leasing company, was looking for secretaries. I applied and was hired. With great pleasure, I bade farewell to the loan company. After about a year, Stearns-Rogers, for some reason I was never privy to, laid off a large number of their employees. I was one of them. As much as I had enjoyed my job at Stearns-Rogers and hated to leave there, luck was with me. United Airlines hired me immediately. I went to work in Hanger Three at Stapleton Field. For the better part of two years, I happily worked in the Design Buildings and Airports Department. It was while there, in the fall of 1950, that I became seriously interested in the State Department's Foreign Service.

The boarding house at 906 Grant was a beautiful old mansion, and I truly loved it. It was built by Colorado railroad pioneer, David Moffet, as a wedding present for his daughter. The Moffett Tunnel, named for David Moffet, was completed in the 1920s. It is a six-mile long tunnel through the Continental Divide with an elevation of more than 9,000 feet. Twice daily, Amtrak's California Zephyr roars through this tunnel, and it remains the most famous and longest railroad tunnel in America.

Mrs. Curdie, our landlady, and I became good friends. She was a strong, no-nonsense lady and a hard worker. She had very strict rules (no men ever allowed except in the common areas, etc.), and we knew not to cross her. There were 18 to 24 girls living at the house. Most of us were working girls, but there were a few students. We spent time together. When it was pay-day Friday, some of us would go to Pagliacci's for a long dinner. It was quite a disappointment when the restaurant closed in 2012. Eating at Pagliacci's is a fond memory of this time in my life.

It was only natural that we would sit around in the evenings and weekends, visiting, gossiping, comparing notes, and telling stories. One of the girls, Catherine Murphy, had in the not too distant past worked as a Foreign Service secretary. She had served in both Warsaw and Moscow. Except for Cathy, none of us had been more than a 1000 miles in any one direction, and most not even that distance. All of us were in awe of Cathy and her experienced travels.

In October 1950, a notice appeared in the *Denver Post*. A recruiting committee of the U.S. State Department would be visiting Denver for three days to recruit for the Foreign Service. Interviews were going to be conducted at the Brown Palace Hotel in downtown Denver on certain days and evenings in November. The article stated, "Anyone interested in becoming a member of the Foreign Service should appear for an interview."

Cathy's roommate, Ruth Toliver, and I immediately decided to apply. There were of course certain criteria to be met and tests to be taken to prove ourselves worthy of becoming a member of this elite Foreign Service in the State Department. Ruth and I dressed up in our Sunday best, hats and all, and made our way to the Brown Palace for the evening interview. Then we waited anxiously for news and instructions for completing the examinations. When instructions did arrive, we quickly did the necessary and sent the examinations to Washington. In early January of 1951, we both were advised of our acceptance and were to report to Washington the first week of February for the six-week training course. At the end of the four weeks, we would again be examined, and if found capable, would receive assignments, then complete the final two weeks of training.

My father, Arley Rudolph, circa 1917

My mother and me, 1929

Morris and me, 1930

Hanging out with Morris, 1934

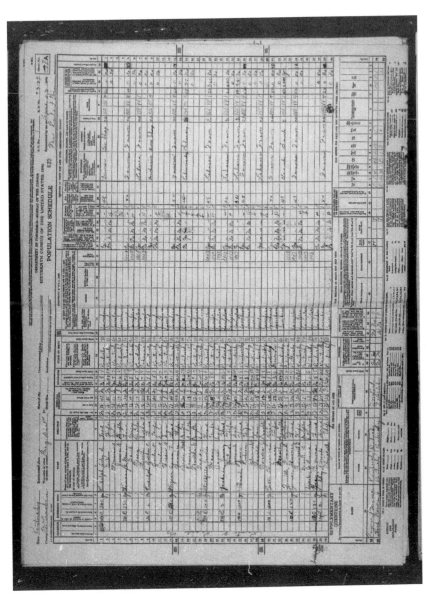

1940 Census record of my family (top four lines)

23

In Washington, 1951

Part II

Sweet, sweet memories you gave-a me, you can't beat the memories you gave-a me, take one fresh and tender kiss, add one stolen night of bliss, one girl, one boy, some grief, some joy, memories are made of this.

From *Memories Are Made of This*

Recorded by Dean Martin in the 1950's.

Washington D.C.

The six weeks in Washington D.C. were intoxicating to say the least. Our intensive training at the Foreign Service Institute (FSI) lasted long hours. Our instructors, though rigid, were grand. There was a constant stream of Foreign Service employees coming and going to and from the four corners of the world. Ruth and I were on our way out into that world.

One of our instructors, Dom Lockwood, was taking evening classes toward his law degree at Georgetown but taught daily at the Foreign Institute. We had a number of different classes, but his class was the one I remember best. I sat in the front row. After two or three days, he came up to me as class was ending and said, "Miss Rudolph, I'd like to see you after class." I was frightened and nervous. *What have I done? What have I said? Will he tell me not to return to class?*

I sat quietly and waited nervously as everyone filed out of the room. Mr. Lockwood came over, smiled, and said, " I would like to invite you out for dinner."

Dom was knowledgeable, polite and serious. He had been at Georgetown law school for two years and was very familiar with Washington. Except for the Foreign Service Institute, we never met during the week days. In the evenings, Dom was busy attending his own classes at Georgetown. But for the next five to six weeks, we took in one or more of the Washington sights each Saturday, and usually on Sundays as well.

In one of my last letters from Washington, I wrote to Mother and David:

> Dom is here now and we are going to get some coffee very soon. Dom is an instructor at the Institute. He is a fine fellow and I know you will like him. I will write later to explain about us. He is going to see me off at the station on Thursday night.

We attended class from eight in the morning until four in the afternoon with a half hour for lunch. They were long days with classes in English, lessons in protocol, and proper manners. Only after receiving my assignment did I learn that Iraq was home to Kurds and Assyrians as well as Iraqis. Most people spoke Arabic as well as their own dialects. We had classes in Arabic, taught by people who had only studied Arabic for a year or so, but I learned little from them.

While in Washington D.C. I attended Mass with a young Foreign Service Officer named Steve and became intrigued by the Catholic Church. Steve was a nice man, and I enjoyed his company, but we were just friends as far as I was concerned.

> Steve and I went to Mass this morning as well as on Friday night. I don't know just when or where it will happen, but I am going to become a Catholic someday. Steve is a wonderful fellow and quite religious. He is very much in love with me and wants me to marry him, but I just think he is a real swell person and that is all.
>
> Maybe by the time I get back, I will be a Catholic and I could take you to church with me. I think you would enjoy it. I do so much.

Besides the training and sightseeing, there was much shopping to be done:

> Yesterday Ruth and I went shopping in Baltimore. We took the train over (about 50 miles from Washington) in the morning and came back in the afternoon. This is what I bought: two cocktail dresses; one, a dress and coat-like affair and is called a duster in beige. The other is black with a cute little pink jacket. Both are of a linen-like material but much more beautiful. I can wear the black dress with the beige duster, so you see, I really have three outfits there. I also bought two cotton wash dresses. One is brown trimmed

in brown gingham, and the other is a very
tiny check in kind of a rust color.
     I also bought a pair of beige, crepe
soled shoes, just sports shoes, six pairs
of nylons, and a pair of rubber boots to
wear over high heels. Of course I have a
million more things to buy. Oh yes, I
bought a real cute little red felt hat with
a black veil which goes over the face to
wear traveling on the plane.

After four weeks of training I was given the choice of Dhahran,
Tel Aviv or Baghdad. In fifth-grade geography, I well remembered
learning about Mesopotamia and how in ancient times this area of the
world was considered the cradle of civilization. It is also an extension
of the Great Rift Valley which runs the width of North Africa and
eventually extends upwards in a northerly direction to encompass the
land between the Tigris and Euphrates Rivers.

Lying in the Kentucky grass, daydreaming as a child, I dreamt of
visiting this place someday where civilization began. Perhaps I would
live there one day.

So I chose Baghdad. Here comes Mesopotamia. Finally!

     Last Thursday I got my passport. It's
really exciting to look at. It has four
visas. A visa is just an admission
certificate to a country. One visa is for
Egypt, another for Syria, another for
Lebanon, and the fourth for Iraq.

February 27, 1951
     Yesterday I was informed that I will
have to fly. I say it this way because no
one *ever* wants to fly to their post. Going

by ship is much more fun, but of course it takes longer, especially where I am going. It takes 18 days by ship to Beirut, which you can see is almost three weeks. I will be leaving on either March 14th or 16th.

So far I have learned a few words relative to the Arabic language, but I am ashamed of myself this week as I have not studied even five minutes. There are so many other things to do and to be taken care of. I am *not* sorry I joined the Foreign Service, but there is one thing I will say—it is certainly not as romantic as one might think before they really get into it, all the things one must contend with and go through before actually getting the post. Still I'm not sorry.

March 1, 1951
Last night I went to a dinner party at the Statler Hotel and met many prominent people, all very wealthy. Among them was the Prime Minister of Bogota, Columbia, S.A. and his wife.

The people who gave the party were Mr. and Mrs. Andrew Higgins from New Orleans. Mr. Higgins[1] is one of the richest men in America. There was another couple there. Believe this or not, they are building a house here; it will have 17 rooms and 7 bathrooms. Can you imagine?!!

---

[1] Andrew Jackson Higgens was famous for building the amphibious LCVPs (landing craft, vehicles, personnel) used in World War II. General Dwight D. Eisenhower credited him with winning the war. "If Higgins had not designed and built those LCVPs, we never could have landed over an open beach. The whole strategy of the war would have been different."

http://en.wikipedia.org/wiki/Andrew_Higgins

Everyone was running about in their mink coats and diamonds galore and there was Jessie with my little old white coat and my beautiful little diamond in black onyx. At first I felt so out of place; then after the first half hour, everyone made me feel as though I belonged there too. They were exceptionally nice to me, and I was happy. Constantly, I kept asking myself, "How can this be? Is it really true?"

Baghdad

On Thursday evening, I boarded the train at Union Station, for the overnight trip to New York. Upon arriving at Grand Central Station, I took a taxi to the KLM office on Fifth Avenue. I can still remember the overwhelmed and overpowered feeling of being surrounded by these gargantuan buildings. That evening we boarded the KLM flight bound for Gander, thence to Shannon Airport in Ireland, then Amsterdam, and arriving in Cairo on the third day. We waited a number of hours before boarding a flight to Baghdad where we arrived early afternoon. It was Sunday, March 18, 1951. At the airport I was met with one of the secretaries, Jean Funck, with an Embassy chauffeur-driven car.

March 16, 1951

Dear Mother and David,

This is written as we leave Gander, Newfoundland. We were here one hour (fuel stop) and it's cold and snowing. The next stop we make, I'll mail this. I think we are stopping in Ireland next. Anyway, I know we arrive in Amsterdam at 8:30 tomorrow but I don't know what time that is your time. We had a perfectly lovely lunch on board. All we could eat served in six courses and believe it or not, champagne with lunch. Really fancy and the food was delicious. They served martinis before dinner.

Draw your own conclusions from this: Right in the middle of lunch, I had to go take my girdle and hose off because I was so miserable from eating so much.

We left New York airport at 12:17 EST and did I ever have an odd feeling. I knew it would be a long, long time before I set foot in the good old U.S.A. again. Please, please don't worry about me. I'm going to be perfectly fine and I'll be back in two years. I'm not dead yet, just going away for a while.

From the airport I was taken to the Semiramis Hotel on Rashid Street. For the next few hours I settled into my room, then was picked up by an Embassy car and taken to dinner at Jean's house. Another secretary or two, as I recall, joined us.

Early the following Monday morning at an appointed time, I was collected from the hotel in an Embassy car and reported to work as the secretary to the Political Officer at the Chancery.

For a region that was the ancient cradle of civilization nestled between the Tigris and Euphrates Rivers, the modern state of Iraq is still young and constantly changing. Following World War I and the collapse of the Ottoman Empire, the British and French governments divided the spoils between them. The U.S. was not silent on this. Under the secret 1916 Sykes-Picot Agreement, Britain took control over most of modern Iraq and maintained indirect control over surrounding areas, while France laid claim to the area that is now known as the country of Syria.

The 1919 Paris Peace Conference and the San Remo Conference in the following year left control of the Middle East largely along the lines of the Sikes-Picot deal but also encouraged the occupying nations to develop locally autonomous governments in the areas they controlled.

For British authorities, charged with organizing the new state of Iraq, the challenge appeared daunting. According to one of the first administrators of the post war region, Sir Arnold Talbot Wilson, "Some 75% of the area was tribal with no tradition of adhering to any central government. Additionally, the former Ottoman officials and military leaders that would likely rule the new state were Sunni in an area which was overwhelmingly Shiite."

Frustrated by the lack of progress made by the British toward promised self-rule, Iraqi religious and political leaders grew angry. Protests broke out throughout the region in the late spring and early summer of 1920. The British moved to quash the growing unrest, arresting scores of tribal and religious leaders. The decision provoked a full-scale revolt with Iraqi militias and bandits launching waves of attacks against the often scattered British outposts.

The rebellion was not universal, but in the cities of Najaf and Karbala the uprising was serious and bloody. It would take thousands of British forces four months to fully quell the violence. In the end some 6,000 Iraqis and 500 British and Indian troops were dead. India was at that time still part of the British Empire, and some of their soldiers fought and died alongside the British.

For the citizens of the emerging nation, the 1920 uprising stood as one of the few unifying events. As Helen Chapin Metz concluded in *Iraq: Issues, Historical Background, Bibliography*, "Al Thawra al-Iraqiya al-Kubra, or the Great Iraqi Revolution (as the 1920 rebellion is called) was a watershed event in contemporary Iraqi history. For the first time, Sunnis and Shias, tribes and cities, were brought together in a common effort."

What the revolt truly triggered was a deep-seated feeling within the British Government that it should limit as much as possible its role in running Iraq. For the British, who in the wake of World War I were focused on limiting the areas in which its war-weary troops and battle-depleted budget extended, the idea of staying in Iraq indeed soured; however, they would maintain a base at Al Habbaniyah until the 1960s. They turned to someone they hoped had popular support and Islamic credentials to come into Iraq to govern—Prince Feisal, the son of Ali Hussein, the Sharif of Mecca, and the leader of the Great Arab Revolt against the Ottomans during World War I. T. E. Lawrence played a major role in this revolt.

In March, 1920, the British crowned Feisal as the first king of Syria, and by July of that year, the kingdom of Syria was abolished by the French Mandate. In August 1921, Feisal was crowned the first king of Iraq. At the same time his brother Abdullah was crowned king of

Jordan. Political and ethnic quarrels have wracked this part of the world ever since.

In *Understanding Iraq,* William Polk, historian, author, (and long-time friend), contends:

> In diplomatic papers passed between London and Delhi in the years before the War, the threat of what was then called "Pan-Islamism" figures prominently. The Allies—Britain, France and Russia—dominated huge Muslim populations in Africa and Asia. Each feared that its subject Muslims might try to drive them out.

The Hashemite Monarchy, which began with Feisal, would govern Iraq until the military coup in 1958, but it was flawed from the start. According to *Iraq: A Country Study,* edited by Helen Chapin Metz for the Library of Congress, 1988:

> Despite his Islamic and pan-Arab credentials, Feisal was not an Iraqi, and no matter how effectively he ruled, Iraqis saw the monarchy as a British creation. The continuing inability of the government to gain the confidence of the people fueled political instability well into the 1970s.

Under the Syles-Picot agreement, the Mosul region was supposed to be controlled by the French, but the British maneuvered it away from them by promising the French Government 25% of the oil revenues from the region. Now the British had to get it away from the new Turkish Government, which also laid claim to it. After lengthy negotiations, the Turks agreed to let the League of Nations settle the matter. In 1925, the body ruled that Mosul with the predominantly Kurdish population was part of Iraq. The League ruled that the Kurds should be given a level of autonomy to govern their own affairs.

The League deal ensured British control of the fledging nation's oil reserves through the UK-dominated Iraqi Petroleum Company (IPC). Under the deal that built the IPC, the Iraqi Government received a small fraction of the revenues from the oil, with the bulk going to a consortium of British, French and American companies.

The agreement lit another long-burning fuse that would lead to future instability in the region. William Polk described the situation in *Understanding Iraq*:

> As younger Iraqis were becoming better educated and were increasingly in contact with European and American sources of information, they began to be aware of the enormous importance of oil in their future. They came to believe that in oil policy, as in other affairs, their government was corrupt and even traitorous.

But with the Mosul deal completed and the Feisal government in charge, the British agreed to grant Iraq full independence in 1932. Iraq joined the League of Nations and emerged as a new nation—yet one with numerous deep rifts within it.

The new Iraq had what many within the country viewed as a *foreign* king. Kurds in the north still strove for independence, and the Shias in the central and southern region chafed under minority Sunni rule. Thusly, the nation of Iraq, cobbled together by the League of Nations and the Colonial Office in London, now faced its own future.

At King Feisal's death in September 1933, his son Ghazi succeeded him, but Ghazi died in a mysterious car crash in April of 1939. Suspicion has it that the Regent Abd al-Ilah, Ghazi's cousin and brother-in-law, was at least partly responsible. Ghazi's son, Feisal II was three years old and his uncle, Prince Abd al-Ilah served as regent, except for a brief period during World War II, until Feisal II came of age and was crowned in May 1953. He kept close ties with the West and although on the surface, it appeared that all was well, under the surface resentments toward the West and the Feisal government simmered.

This was the convoluted Iraq I flew into on March 18,1951.

Embassy Life

When leaving for Baghdad, I knew little about the Middle East other than what I'd learned in fifth-grade geography class along with the preparatory classes at the FSI in Washington. Even though civilization in Baghdad goes back 10,000 years, I don't recall visiting museums or taking an interest in the political or cultural history. What I remember about life at the American Embassy was party after party. It was just the greatest time.

The Embassy compound consisted of three buildings: the Chancery, the Counselor of Embassy's residence, and a security office. The Chancery, a small replica of the White House in Washington, D.C., was the main building. It housed the Ambassador's Residence and Office, Office of the Counselor of Embassy, Office of the Political Attaché, as well as the Administrative Office. The Commercial Attaché's Office was located in a different building about a quarter of a mile away.

A three-legged gazelle roamed the garden that serviced all three of the buildings. The quite-tame gazelle was a present given to Mrs. Crocker, the Ambassador's wife.

On my first day, after being introduced to the staff, I accompanied the sergeant, who picked up the mail, and was taken to the Military Attaché Office to meet each and every one there. This office was located about a half mile from the Embassy compound. At the Attaché Office all three branches of service (Air Force, Army and Navy) were represented. I didn't remember any of the names of the people I met that first day but certainly would soon come to know them well!

There were times my presence was requested at dinner in the Ambassador's Residence to fill in as the extra lady. For me, this was an honor. It could be my friend Pat (secretary to the Commercial Attaché) or me—usually it was me. The first time the Ambassador's secretary, Florence Neverman, summoned me to dinner at the Residence on such and such date and time (no more than two days in advance) I responded, "But I have a date." Her retort was, "You do not say 'No' to the Ambassador. You will be there." I was.

The mail arrived by pouch through Cairo from the Secretary of State's office in Washington. Of course in those days we didn't have cell phones or the internet. Everything was done by mail or teletype— high priority messaging. There were some phone calls, but it was very difficult to arrange a call. One needed to register and wait two or three days before the call could take place, and then it may not happen. All

Foreign Service employees could receive personal mail through the pouch. It arrived twice weekly by courier from Cairo. I did receive letters from Dom, my instructor at the FSI, but soon forgot him and started dating the Cairo courier. When the courier came to Baghdad each Tuesday and Friday, we had a standing date to go dancing at Abdullah's, the only night club in Baghdad.

At that time there were seven single girls working for the American Embassy in Baghdad. Four of us were in the Chancery: the Ambassador's secretary; the Counselor of Embassy's secretary; the Political Officer's secretary (myself) and the Administrative Officer's secretary. Then there were a Communications Office secretary, the Commercial Attaché's secretary (this was my friend Pat), and last but not least, was the United States Information Service (USIS) secretary. The USIS was located a few miles away in a downtown office.

Of course there were single fellows in the Chancery and certainly at the Attaché Office. Dating was no problem for any of us. Cathy Murphy, the girl in Denver who was responsible for getting Ruth and me interested in the Foreign Service, had worked for Ambassador Crocker when she was in Warsaw. He was now our Ambassador. His present secretary, Florence Neverman, had also been with him in Warsaw.

The Commercial Attaché was giving a cocktail party at the Alwiyah Club the Monday evening after my arrival. Everyone was invited. I met Costa, my future husband, that night, but of course didn't know it. I was still jet lagged, confused and all agog. My surroundings had become completely different from anything I'd seen before in my life. If anyone at the Embassy gave a party, usually the entire Embassy family was invited (no children naturally.) There were about 40 employees at the Embassy and Attaché Office, but if spouses and children were included, the number went up to around 125.

For about six weeks it was total excitement—the work, meetings, any and all connected to the Embassy. Immediately I joined *the* Club, The Alwiyah Club. It was predominately a British club; however the members represented most all of the diplomatic missions in Baghdad. This was not totally a foreigner's club. Many prominent Iraqis were also members, as well as various and sundry other nationalities. Most of my friends that summer were English, and I came to know them well.

One afternoon at the pool, I spotted Mrs. Crocker, complete with hat and gloves, in a corner of the lawn surrounding the pool. Having tea with her was a tall and very good-looking man in his bathing suit. She called out to me, "Hello, Miss Rudolph," and proceeded to introduce me. "Miss Rudolph, you must meet Mr. Byroade, our Secretary of State."

We both said, "How do you do," and shook hands.

Henry Byroade did not seem particularly impressed with me, as I recall. (What would Henry Byroade possibly have in common with an insignificant secretary at the Embassy?) A "Miss Rudolph" was the last thing he was interested in. It did not surprise me later when I learned more of his reputation and discovered he was never considered the most popular or effective Secretary of State.

In those days at the Embassy, we were driven anywhere we wished or needed to go. If we didn't have someone to drive us, we would ask for, and a car would be sent. We were picked up and brought to and from work in an Embassy car. The summer hours were from seven a.m. to two p.m. with no break. Instead of having the car drive me home after work, I'd go to the Club. Everyone—well almost—congregated there. There was a swimming pool, tennis courts, a dining room, and a bar with a dart board. Saturday night was dance night with a live orchestra.

By mid-April the outdoor life of garden parties, swimming, and tennis began in Baghdad, and of course the Club. At that time, only one apartment building existed in the entire city, called the Embassy Apartments, but it was not in any way affiliated with the Embassy. Most everybody lived in houses or villas with sizable gardens all surrounded by high walls. During the summer months, entertainment happened in the gardens of homes.

I met Nadir at the Alwiyah Club. Having been friends with his half-sister Majda he and I became good buddies. Nadir was near to my age and was part Circassian[2]. He was fair skinned with blue eyes and fair hair. We swam together for about a month that summer. After swimming, almost daily, we would go to the Suk (bazaar) and rummage around in the shops to see what we could find. We rarely bought much of anything but laughed a lot and had fun. At six o'clock, we'd go back to the Club, get a bite to eat and swim again, or go dancing. I lived within walking distance of the Club, and if I had a date, he would walk me home, or I could ask for an Embassy car. Of course this only happened if the Cairo Courier was not in town.

Many years later, while in Jeddah, I had gone to the bazaar which at that time was located in the old section of the city. While strolling through the winding paths, I came upon an antique shop. Inside there were two men dressed in Arab regalia. Looking at one of them, I

---

[2] The Circassians are a North Caucasian ethnic group native to Circassia, who were displaced in the course of the Russian conquest of the Caucasus in the 19th century, especially after the Russian–Circassian War in 1864. The term "Circassian" includes the Adyghe (Circassian:Adyge) and Kabardian people.

http://en.wikipedia.org/wiki/Circassians

recognized Nadir. We spent a few minutes chatting and catching up. It was a delightful encounter. I never saw him again.

One would think I never worked, but I did. Not only was I the political secretary but also became the first Point Four Program secretary. The Point Four Program provided assistance to needy countries around the world and was created and developed during the Truman Administration.

I lived with the Makiya family. Margaret was English and her husband was Iraqi. They had two young children and lived in an area known as the Alwiyah Bungalows. It was a group of low houses that had been built during World War I as British officers' quarters. They were spacious one story dwellings surrounded by high walls with huge gardens in front and circle driveways. The Bungalows were numbered—I think there were eighteen in all—and the area was patrolled nightly by guards.

My private quarters consisted of a very large room and a bathroom in a joined-on area of the main house with its own entrance. The cook served me separately in my own quarters.

No one had air conditioning in those days, but the Bungalows, and of course my quarters, were cooled by an *agoul* that was very effective. The windows were totally covered on the outside with branches from the camel-thorn shrub woven into a frame. Above this frame was a narrow pipe with small holes that extended the width at the top of the window. Water flowed through the pipe and dripped down on the window covering to the ground providing coolness through the windows.

This was home for me, and it felt very safe. Margaret Makiya was nice enough, but she kept her distance. It was there that I met Farida on a Sunday afternoon. She was 12 years old at the time and was out walking in the garden. Farida's mother Toni was visiting with her friend Margaret. I saw this pretty young girl and went outside to say hello. She'd been playing with Margaret's children, perhaps became bored, and came out into the garden to look at the flowers. We became friends and have remained friends all these years. She now lives in London.

Around the middle of May, I became despondent and discouraged. Frank Allen, the Political Officer and my boss, was extremely impatient and demanding. It seemed I could do nothing to please him. He constantly harassed me about my work, not remembering nor thinking that I was not only young, but this was my first post as a Foreign Service employee. I had much, very much to learn. Once he gave me invitations to prepare for an event he and his wife were hosting. I knew no better and typed them up very nicely. He stiffly reprimanded me, "Don't you know you don't type invitations? They *must* be hand written!" Maybe this is something I should have known or learned in Washington, but I didn't. To this day I cringe if I see a typed invitation.

Frank Allen made my life so miserable that I was all but ready to resign and leave, but I decided to give myself six months. Fortunately for me, around the first of June, Frank Allen was transferred. He was replaced by someone much more patient and understanding. The new Political Officer and his wife, the Ambassador's secretary (but not his wife yet at the time) ended up becoming dear friends for years to come.

There were some interesting personnel at the embassy. Wilber "Bill" Crane Eveland was stationed there from 1950-1952 as the Assistant Army Attaché. Bill Eveland went on to write the controversial memoir[3], *Ropes of Sand,* a study of what the CIA did wrong in the Middle East. For some people, Bill's opinions were somewhat questionable.

In mid-summer, 1951, the arrival of William "Bill" Polk in Baghdad was an event about which the Embassy had been well-advised. Bill had driven from Beirut, where he had spent a number of months studying Arabic. This was an event because in those days it was not the norm for an American to be driving to Baghdad, across the desert, through Syria and Jordan, then on to Iraq.

About noontime, on the specified day, a small black Ford coupe pulled into the Embassy Compound. Bill Polk had arrived, and he was well received. Soon, he was directed to the Embassy Apartments where he would be living for his approximate six-month stay in Baghdad.

Of course I knew who Bill was from his heralded arrival at the Embassy in 1951, but Bill's and Costa's friendship began when they met on the *Marine Corp* ship in 1946. Bill, a relative of the president, James Polk, was 17 years old when he came first to Iraq with Costa, newly graduated from the New Mexico Military Institute. When they arrived in Iraq, my husband invited him to stay with him and his parents. Bill remained with the Halkias family for six months.

Undoubtedly, Bill soon contacted Costa when he arrived in Baghdad in 1951. Personally, I saw Bill no more than a time or two during his visit. Perhaps he saw Costa a number of times; I do not know. It was only in later years that I came to understand the depth of their friendship. They were truly close friends.

In those days, the U.S. Government maintained Attaché planes (DC3's) for both the Air Force and Navy, at major diplomatic missions throughout the world. Baghdad, being a major mission, was privileged

---

[3] See reviews of *Ropes of Sand* on Amazon.com

with two planes. These planes were flown out of Baghdad about once a month by the Air Force Colonel, the Navy Commander, or a Marine Colonel. A destination could be Beirut, Dhahran, Addis Ababa, or Frankfurt, and sometimes Aviano, a base in northeastern Italy. The nearer bases, Beirut or Dhahran, were usually one-day trips. Other and further locations were three or four-day trips. Sometimes one or two of the Embassy personnel would get invited for a trip.

The highlight of my summer occurred in July when I was invited to travel on the Air Attaché plane to Beirut for the day. Now that was special! I had even been allowed/invited into the cockpit for the Beirut landing. Piloted by Colonel Tommy Summers and his crew, we took off early in the morning for Beirut where we spent a grand day shopping and sightseeing. We had a wonderful lunch at the Lucullus Restaurant next to the Sea, near where the Phoenicia Hotel now stands. It was love at first sight, and I've been in love with Beirut ever since.

Costa

Here with a Loaf of Bread beneath the Bough,
A flask of wine, a Book of Verse—and Thou
Beside me singing in the wilderness—
And Wilderness is Paradise enow.

Omar Khayám, *The Rubáiyát*

49

Costa's parents

Costa

Costa as a young boy in Chios,
circa 1927

Costa and his father on a shooting trip in
Northern Iraq, circa 1938

Ralph Haddad, Costa, and Vincent Asfar after a successful partridge
shoot, circa 1951

Although I had met Costa at the Commercial Attaché's cocktail party the day after arriving in Baghdad, he didn't ask me out until a few months later. We often said hello at the Alwiyah Club and occasionally at parties. Costa was well-liked, well-known, highly respected, and a successful business man. When someone from the Embassy or one of the small number of Americans from outside the Embassy community had a question, they would always call on Costa. He was good-looking, intelligent, well-traveled and fun to be with. He understood the different peoples of the Middle East extremely well and how they related to each other. When he did invite me out, I was surprised that he was interested in me. However, I did not hesitate to say yes.

It was August. I had been in Baghdad almost five months, and we saw each other daily for the next ten weeks. One evening, while his mother and sister were in Europe, he invited another couple and me to his home for a game of bridge and dinner. Costa's mother loved cats, and there were four or five of them that roamed around the large garden. Sarkis, the family servant, was serving us dinner in the garden. Suddenly, I looked up and saw a cat flying off the end of Costa's arm. He threw that cat off the table like it was a fly. I think he was mortified, but no one spoke a word. We went ahead eating as if nothing had happened.

Costa was 28 years old (he would turn 29 the following February), and I have always believed that he felt he should be married by the time he was 30. In mid-October we drove to Beirut and planned to marry in the Greek Orthodox Church. Upon arrival, he called his Greek Orthodox friend, Mr. Nahra, and asked if he could arrange for the Bishop to marry us.

"I will go and meet the Bishop and see what he says." A few hours later, Mr. Nahra phoned to say, "I met the Bishop, and he wants $10,000 to marry you."

"No, thank you," was Costa's response. "I will *not* give him $10,000. I will give him $1,000."

The following day, Nahra called and said, "The Bishop will marry you for $1,000."

So we were married at the Greek Orthodox Cathedral, and to this day I often pass by this church when in Beirut.

What can I say? Here's what I know for certain: When a person remains for a long period of time in an ultra-unfamiliar environment, far from home, he or she often loses perspective, takes giant steps, makes rash decisions, all of which would never happen if that person remains in his or her own familiar environment.

I took that giant step.

Sometime in November, after we were secretly married in Beirut, I was approached by Phillip Ireland, the Counselor of the Embassy. "It is common knowledge that you are dating Costa Halkias. I hope you don't do anything foolish." I assured him I wouldn't. Because I was working with classified information at the Embassy, I could not marry an *alien*. For some bureaucratic reason, Costa's passport had been withdrawn for a short period of time, but this did not worry me, because I knew it was going to be easily corrected. When it was put in order shortly thereafter, I remember saying, "What a wonderful Christmas present."

Costa was christened Constantine John Halkias, for his grandfather. He was of Greek-Armenian descent, and his mother called him Costa (as in the *cost* of tea.) So did I. Sometime in the 1980s, certain persons started calling him John. We of course had our own young John. I never knew what brought this name change about, but to me he was always Costa.

Costa's mother Eugenie was Armenian, born in Izmir (Smyrna), a city on the western coast of Turkey. I do not know from where in Armenia Eugenie's parents came before they arrived in Izmir, or the reason for their moving on to Baghdad when Eugenie was a child, but the family name was Minassian. Perhaps her father saw the handwriting on the wall, because in 1922, Izmir was destroyed by Mustapha Kemal Atatürk[4]. In any case, Eugenie, at the age of 14 years old, was sent to Nainital in India to study with English nuns for three years. At an early age, she learned to speak Turkish, Armenian, English, Arabic, and French; she was proficient in all five languages. At the age of 17, when she returned to Baghdad, Eugenie, being a very pretty young blonde and blue-eyed woman, soon married my father-in-law. She became skilled in her sixth language, Greek.

I never knew Costa's father, John Constantine. He was born on the island of Chios, one of the Cyclades Islands, in the Aegean Sea, either in 1891 or 1892. As a young man, he fought in the war between Greece and Turkey in the early 1900s when the Ottoman Empire was breaking up, before and during World War I. Costa's father was a foot soldier in the Greek army which invaded Turkey. He was one of the fortunate ones. Thousands and thousands of the soldiers either starved

---

[4] "On Saturday, September 9, 1922, the victorious Turkish cavalry rode into Smyrna, the richest and most cosmopolitan city in the Ottoman Empire. The city's vast wealth created centuries earlier by powerful Levantine dynasties, its factories teemed with Greeks, Armenians, Turks, and Jews. Together, they created a majority Christian city that was unique in the Islamic World. But to the Turkish nationalists, Smyrna was a city of infidels."

Paradise Lost: *Smyrna, 1922* by Giles Milton

or froze to death during this war. Those who survived returned home barefoot and in rags.

Sometime after John Constantine left the army, he took a ship to Alexandria in Egypt, undoubtedly to *seek his fortune*. He quickly decided he did not like that city, even though for many long years there had been a large Greek population in Alexandria. He remained only a few months, then boarded another ship which would take him to Bombay where his older sister Irene was living. John stayed only a year or so in India and decided to come to Iraq. First, he stopped off in Basrah, the port of Iraq, but eventually ended up in Baghdad. He managed what was known as the Royal Cinema for about five years, saved his money, and opened up his own business selling sporting arms and home appliances.

Costa's grandparents, Papou and YiaYiá, were originally from Kardamyla, a town in the northeastern part of Chios. The Island of Chios is much nearer to Turkey than to mainland Greece. Turkish influence is prevalent, as is Venetian, on the island. Many of the old buildings, especially private homes, retain a Venetian flavor, including the house which was eventually owned by Costa. This house was built by the Venetians in the late 1500s or early 1600s.

It has always been commonly known that the Cambos was the richer area of the island. Therefore, in the early 1900s when the opportunity arose, Papou did not hesitate to leave Kardamyla, moving his wife and six children (John, Therodora, Niko, George, Irene, and Mike) to a better life.

The Cambos is a green valley south of Chora (Chios Town) covered primarily with citrus groves and is also considered one of the most beautiful areas of the island. Papou came as a sharecropper to the house and garden owned by a certain Englishman, Mr. Perthwaite, who resided in the city of Izmir, Turkey. After moving to the Cambos, two more children, Demosthenes and Marianthe, were born.

Eventually, John, Nico, and George emigrated to Baghdad. Demo and Mike went to America but returned to Chios after a few years. Uncles always called it "Amurica"—never "the States." In the meantime, Theodora, the eldest daughter, died. Irene, the second eldest daughter, married Socrate Moschovis, and went off to Bombay in India with her husband where they remained for many years. The youngest daughter Marianthe married Apostolos Stravanaki, a White Russian, and lived the remainder of her life in Athens.

In 1937, Papou died, and Mike and Demos had returned to Chios. Around this time, Costa's father John bought the property from Mr. Perthwaite. This gave his mother and two brothers, Mike and Demo, their own home.

When John Constantine died in 1948, ownership of the property in Chios passed directly to Costa. Of course there was inheritance tax to be paid. Living in Baghdad, Costa had no money in Greece. What to do?

This is the story of how the inheritance tax was paid: Costa had a pair of shoes with thick heels. He drilled four holes in each heel, filled each hole with King George gold pounds purchased in Baghdad, went to Beirut on the Nairn bus and boarded a ship to Piraeus, the Port of Athens. There he changed the gold coins into drachmas and boarded another ship bound for Chios. He was happily on his way to pay the inheritance tax on his house. He arrived with two very sore legs from carrying those coins in his heels. Thus Costa became the proud owner of the property at Talaros in the Cambos on the island of Chios.

On the three-day boat trip from Beirut to Athens, I wonder, *did he sleep with his shoes on?*

Talaros is no more than a street corner about a half mile away from the house, where there is a small ouzo factory owned by the Teteris Brothers. Ouzo, a clear and colorless, anise-flavored and Greek liqueur is distilled there. When ouzo is mixed with water, it turns white. I am told that the Teteris Brothers make excellent ouzo—certainly Mohamed, our cook could well vouch for Teteris ouzo!

When Costa was four years old, his parents took him to the island of Chios to live with his grandparents and uncles, Mike and Demos, in the 300-year-old house. This was the same house Costa and I eventually came back to, remodeled in 1976-1978, and spent many lovely summers there with our children.

Costa remained with his grandparents and uncles for three years, until the age of seven. While on the Island, he learned Greek very well, sang in the church choir, and attended early school. I do not know if his parents visited him while he was there, but it is doubtful. Upon returning to Baghdad, he entered the American school where he studied through the eighth grade. From there he enrolled in Baghdad College, a high school founded in 1933, by American Jesuits. He did very well, graduating at the age of seventeen. He was accepted as a sophomore at M.I.T. in Boston; however, his father decided that he should study radio engineering in New York instead. Father was the boss.

In September of 1940, 17-year-old Costa boarded a ship in Basrah (Iraq) to begin the journey to the United States. War was raging in the Atlantic, and the only way from that area to the States was to travel through the Pacific. The ship was a cargo with holding space for a dozen passengers. Among the passengers was the Sheridan family from Cairo, who had boarded in Alexandria. Costa became well acquainted with the parents, two teen-aged children, Joe and Yvonne, and the grandmother on the three-month journey aboard the ship. They docked in Portland, Oregon on December 7, 1940, where Costa disembarked. He made his way across country by train to New York. The ship continued on to San Francisco—Sheridans and all.

Some years would pass before Costa renewed his friendship with young Joe Sheridan, but finally it did happen, and our families became very close through the coming years. We spent many happy times together in Beirut and Cairo, as well as in Athens, Cyprus, and London.

When Costa graduated from Engineering School in 1944, even though he was not a U.S. citizen, he was drafted into the U.S. Army. He told the Induction Officer, "I do not want to go to the Army; I want to go into the Navy." Permission was granted. He spent two happy years in the Navy: boot camp at the Great Lakes, training in upstate New York near the Finger Lakes, and in the Ozarks in Arkansas, a month in Washington D.C., and last but not least, the second and final year in Hawaii.

All in all, Costa much enjoyed his time in the Navy and would say so with pride. He had left Baghdad in 1940 and would not return until he was discharged in 1946. He did return to Baghdad as a CIA operative attached to the U.S. Embassy, incognito of course. He remained with the CIA until the summer of 1958. I never knew of his connection with the CIA until a week before we were married, when he sat me down and told me. I was taken by surprise. As far as I knew, he was a business man, representing a number of American and English firms, no more, no less.

I accepted what he told me and never inquired nor did I ever know about this side of his life. While living in Baghdad, about once a week someone would come to our house from the political section of the Embassy, often remaining with Costa for two or three hours. They would talk. I suppose he was imparting information of importance; I do not know. My only duty was to offer coffee along with cookies, pie, cake, or whatever my kitchen produced, and hurry out of the room. They would sit and do what they needed to do in privacy. I knew all these people and their wives well, as we were in touch socially for all the years we were in Baghdad.

My husband had a brilliant mind. He spoke five languages fluently: Arabic, Armenian, Greek, French and English. His Arabic and English were excellent, but Arabic was probably his best language. He spoke most of the dialects of the Middle East well. Costa was a master at putting business deals together. In later years, I thought many times that if he had made a profession of connecting companies, for a price of course, and then moving on to the next project, life would have been much easier for him and his family. But he loved commerce and always wanted to be involved in the day to day affairs. He thrived on and loved the bargaining and selling that went along with business in the Middle East.

Costa wrote beautiful letters but it was not always easy for me to talk to him in person. More often than not, he did not share his thoughts with me. One day while sitting on the terrace in Chios with our daughter Penny, I said to her, "Many times I just never know what Daddo is thinking." She answered me, "If you know what Daddo is thinking, you would know as much as he knows. You can never know."

Many times mothers-in-law are not easy on their daughters-in-law. Eugenie fell into that category. She had her own ideas and plans in mind for Costa. They did not include this American girl working at the American Embassy. She would have very much preferred one of the nice Armenian girls of Baghdad. Well, her son had his own ideas. Not only did he marry the wrong girl, he married at the wrong time. In the Middle East, at that time and era, a brother (whether he was younger or older, it didn't matter) never married before his sisters had wed. For those reasons, I never became Eugenie's favored one.

Even though Eugenie and the sisters, Maria and Thalia, had been and were often traveling in Europe, their home was still Baghdad. Coincidentally, Eugenie and Maria returned to Beirut while Costa and I were there to be married in October, 1951. He arranged for us to meet his mother and sister for an afternoon tea on the terrace of the St. George Hotel. At the meeting, only then did he tell them we were going to be married. I said nothing.

Maria immediately asked, "When are you going to go live in America?"

Costa answered, "We are not going to live in America; we will be living in Baghdad."

"Oh," she said.

Neither of Costa's sisters were ever particularly fond of his wife. They showed little sense of humor—with me anyway—and it was not always easy being in their company. Joking or teasing could easily be taken the wrong way. Their moods could change with the wind, and I was never sure what would happen from one moment to the next.

Maria was a year younger than Costa, and Thalia five years younger than Maria. Thalia, a very pretty girl, was named for the Greek Goddess of music, song, and dance. She had a wonderful mezzo-soprano voice, and Costa as the head of the family encouraged and constantly promoted her talents. Thalia was in Rome studying at St. Cecelia's the summer of 1951; it was from there that my mother-in-law and Maria had come when I first met them in Beirut in October of that year.

Before going to Rome, Thalia had spent two years at the London Conservatory of Music. So her second round of training was at St. Cecilia's where she remained for two more years. After Rome, she entered the Julliard School of Music in New York. Because she was blessed with a beautiful voice, Costa desperately wanted her to make the best use of her talents. However, while in New York, Thalia met a young man from São Paulo. They were married and moved to Curitiba in Brazil, where they lived for five years. There were no children, and when they divorced, she returned to Athens where her mother and sister were then living.

In the summer of 1951, on the return trip from visiting Thalia in Rome, Maria met a young merchant marine officer named Vassily Spiropoulos. Two years later, in 1953, they were married. They had one son and two daughters, but the youngest daughter died young. Vassily later retired from the Greek Navy and became a successful businessman in Athens. Both Costa and I got along well with him. He was an all-right fellow. Maria, Vassily, and their son have all passed away. Her daughter, Margie, is the only one left in Maria's family. She no longer stays in touch with us.

Through the years, Thalia had nervous breakdown after nervous breakdown. At times she would come to Beirut, and time and again would need hospital treatment. Costa made trip after trip to Athens on her behalf, taking her to doctors and hospitals here and there. This went on for years and years. Even my adult children, John and Katherine, made a trip to Athens to see and be with her in 2009. A few months after they returned to the States, Thalia committed suicide. John and Katherine went back to Athens to assist at her burial.

While living in Denver as well as in Washington D.C., I had friends who were Catholic, and I strongly considered becoming a Catholic myself. Upon arrival in Baghdad, I quickly discovered Baghdad College, the Jesuit School. Each Saturday afternoon, there was a baseball game on the school grounds. Certain Embassy and military personnel pitted themselves against the priests for a lively game. These games were well attended by both Embassy personnel and families, as well as most of the priests, and it was always an enjoyable afternoon.

In the early summer of 1951, I began instructions with Father Joseph P. Merrick, S.J., a Boston Jesuit, and one of the early instructors at Baghdad College. By late summer, I was baptized into the Catholic Church.

Even though we had married in the Greek Orthodox Church, I surely wanted to marry in the Catholic Church. Costa had spent five years with the Jesuits and knew them all well. He had no problem marrying again in the Catholic Church. Thus we were married on January 16, 1952, in the little chapel at Baghdad College. Ambassador Crocker graciously gave me away, and a reception for about 125 people was held at the Alwiyah Club.

The following day we flew to Beirut to attend the wedding of some friends. The second day we left for Nicosia. We rented a small Morris Minor to travel about Cyprus where we enjoyed many of the ancient sights. After a week, we returned to Beirut for an overnight stay and then back to Baghdad.

Ambassador Crocker giving me away

Only when you drink from the river of silence shall you begin to sing. And when you have reached the mountaintop, then you shall begin to climb.

Khalil Gibran

Costa and me on our wedding day, January 16, 1952

John Constantine

Your children are not your children.
They are the sons and daughters of Life's longing for itself.

Kahlil Gibran

Shortly after our Catholic wedding, in January, 1952, the State Department chose to send Costa to the States during the coming summer for a three-month training program, both in Chicago and New York. Our first born child was expected in August. Therefore, it was decided I would leave Baghdad in late May; Costa would leave in June. I was to remain in Moline, Illinois with my mother until he was free to visit. His training would be six weeks in Chicago and another six weeks in New York.

In early August while Costa was in Chicago, I had gone there by train for a weekend visit. That weekend, Johnny made his appearance. The birth turned into an emergency, but it worked out very well: great doctor, great hospital, and excellent care. Costa said, "I want all my children to be born in the States." But it didn't happen that way. The baby and I stayed with Costa in Chicago until he completed his six weeks training.

Although they were living in Moline, Mother and David had gone to the family home in Kentucky for a visit. When Costa completed his training in Chicago, Mother suggested I bring Johnny to Kentucky so she might care for him while we were to be in New York for the next six weeks, before returning to Baghdad. I was in full agreement and immediately left for Kentucky with him. I would return to New York, and this would give Costa and me some time to ourselves. It was not to be. After a week of caring for Johnny, my step-father, David, phoned and said Mother was having a nervous breakdown and I must come and collect my son. Immediately, and as quickly as possible, I was on the next plane there. Staying one night, I returned to New York the following day with Johnny, feeling angry and disappointed with both Mother and David.

When Costa's training in New York was completed, we took Pan Am to Beirut. However, before leaving New York, I wanted to buy a mink stole—they were all the rage in those days. Costa did not object, but said if I got the mink stole we would take coach back to Beirut. That was okay with me, and the mink stole was bought. We flew first class anyway back to the Middle East. By then it was early October.

We stopped in Beirut before returning to Baghdad. Staying in the old downtown Normandy Hotel, we took Johnny with us each day to either the Bain Militaire or the San Simone beach. The weather was beautiful, and there were few people swimming. It was warm, not hot, and the water was perfect, as always in October. It was a lovely week at the beach.

From Beirut, we took the inaugural flight of the first jet plane operated by Middle East Airlines (Air Liban) to Baghdad. In those days nothing was said about *inaugural flights*; however, when an airline receives permission to fly into a new destination, the airline invites guests (free of course) who are important to the company to fly on the first flight. Even though we were not necessarily important for the Airline, we were booked on the flight and went along as regular paying customers. We arrived home in late October 1952 and settled back into life in Baghdad with our new son.

Jean, my good friend had earlier in the year married Ralph Barrow, the Political Attaché, and replaced Florence Neverman as secretary to Ambassador Crocker. She and I were unhappy with the Baghdad bread, and we often discussed the making of yeast bread. For some time I had intended to try my hand at this, so we embarked on a bread-making crusade. Now when I travel to Beirut, I bring back Arabic bread!

Jean had already proudly produced, perhaps once or twice, some white bread. On this particular morning after Costa had gone to the office as usual, I proceeded to make up a batch of dough and left it to rise.

Johnny was three and a half months old now. Just before midnight I had given him a bottle of milk and did not expect him to wake too early. He usually awoke by seven or seven thirty, but it was now just before eight and not a sound from the nursery. He slept in a carriage because his bed and other furniture, having been shipped from the States, had not yet arrived. When I entered the room and pulled down his blanket, his little body was cold and stiff. I knew he was dead. Like a mad person I rushed to the phone and called Costa. He arrived in a flash. I was waiting for him at the front gate. He ran into the house, grabbed Johnny, and we jumped back into the car with our driver, Abdullah, and *flew* to the nearest hospital. He was examined, his lungs were pumped, but he was dead. It was called crib death; nothing could be done to change it. We returned home with his little body.

Costa phoned our pediatrician friend, Dr. Diran Kouyoumdjian, who arrived in minutes. He of course gave us the same pronouncement. I phoned Jean who literally ran the two miles from their house to us. Another dear friend, Carrie Gleason, had heard the news which seemed to have traveled like wildfire throughout the Embassy family. She also soon arrived with Scott, her two-month-old son. Both Carrie and Jean were there for me that day as well as in the days to come. Costa also called our dear friend Father Merrick who soon arrived to be with us.

By noontime a small coffin appeared. Costa washed and dressed Johnny in a little white dress and white booties. He wore a small gold cross and a little gold bracelet. Together, we laid him inside the little wooden box.

At two p.m. we were at the grave in the Catholic Cemetery where a graveside service was held on November 19, 1952. Father Merrick officiated at the service. It was raining, but almost the entire adult Embassy family was present.

During the months of my instructions to become a Catholic in 1951, I became good friends with three of the nuns at the Chapel of the Sisters of Presentation, the Catholic girls' school at Bab al-Shargi, where Father Merrick served as the Sunday priest. This school was sort of a mid-way point between Baghdad College and the American Embassy, and it was only natural that Father Merrick gave me instructions at the girls school. This chapel would become my church throughout my Baghdad days.

Sister Joseph, an American; Sister Dominica, who was French, and the elder, and Sister Gabrielle from England, always moved as a trio outside their school. They were dear to me, and I even felt to a certain extent, they were my protectors.

The day following Johnny's death, these three nuns appeared early at our front door. I had not expected them but was deeply touched and humbled. In my usual way, I offered coffee and cookies which they graciously accepted. The visit was not lengthy, and soon we joined hands in prayer led by Sister Gabrielle. At the end she turned and said to me, "God needed another rose for His garden."

In 2004, during the U.S. war in Iraq, when I discovered a young friend of ours was being sent to Baghdad, I asked him to look up Johnny's grave. He sent me pictures. The grave had been destroyed and emptied; the protective grave plaque was broken and scattered.

When, in early 2006, the gravestone for Costa was set, a smaller one, 'In Memory Of' was placed next to Costa's grave that reads: John

Constantine Halkias, born in Chicago, Illinois, August 2, 1952, died in Baghdad, Iraq, November 18, 1952, with the inscription, "God needed another rose for His garden."

Penelope Anne

They come through you but not from you,
And though they are with you yet they belong not to you.

Kahlil Gibran

For our first year of marriage, we lived in an older rented house in Baghdad. In January of 1953, Costa announced to me that he intended to build a house for us on a piece of land he owned. The property was near the American Embassy as well as near his mother's home.

He engaged an architect, a builder and in late January broke ground for our future home. The plot or garden as it was called was a piece of land his father had purchased a number of years earlier to be divided between Costa's younger sister Thalia and himself. Thus Costa laid claim to his half and the building began. It took almost six months to complete. On July Fourth, we moved from the small rental house to our own home. The house was not the largest but was very comfortable with four bedrooms, two bathrooms, dining room, large kitchen and store room. There was a fireplace in the sunken living room, as well as the dining room.

In those days, Baghdad had no furniture stores. As we wanted new furniture for our new house, it was necessary to have it made by a local carpenter or import from abroad. What we didn't have made locally, we ordered from Sears and Roebuck. Because Costa was determined to have a nice kitchen, which almost no one had, he ordered a complete kitchen consisting of cupboards and all appliances from the States. I was one of the first of only a few persons in Baghdad to sport an electric stove. Kerosene stoves were the rule of the day at that time, and as long as the wicks were kept clean, they worked fine. Friends coming to visit us in our new home were primarily interested in checking out the kitchen, and I will say were duly impressed.

I became the proud owner of a used Singer sewing machine and somehow acquired a sewing manual. Even though my mother was an expert seamstress, I knew next to nothing about stitching anything

73

together. With this instruction book, I made drapes (lined of course!) and curtains for the entire house. Next came the bedspreads. After two or three months, I considered myself an accomplished seamstress. Excellent fabrics were available to work with; when I finished, all our windows, even the storeroom windows, and the beds were beautifully dressed.

We bought Persian rugs, Kermans. The rugs are woven with a warp (lengthwise) and a weft (crosswise) thread, and we carefully placed the rugs in a manner to show off the colors. They were cleaned daily with a broom made of palm fronds, and once a year, the rugs were taken up to the flat roof where they were washed and hung to dry on the parapet, the low wall that enclosed the roof.

Costa always delighted in flowers—all kinds of flowers. He ordered rose bushes from both England and France. We even had a Princess Grace rose bush. There were bulbs from Holland and seeds from Burpee in the U.S. He exchanged ideas, cuttings and the like with friends and engaged a full-time gardener named Sahib. Each morning and evening Costa's delight was to make an inspection tour of the garden.

Our garden was surrounded by a high brick wall three meters (about 10 ft.) high, as were all houses in the Middle East. We held many parties outside in the garden, as did everyone else. Along the entire wall within and the entire compass of the garden were about 20 date trees. All in all, there are 120 varieties of dates, some better than others and only a few varieties are favored. Two of our trees were *his* and *hers*. The Bourbon (mine) were large black dates and the Burhee (his) were smaller brown ones. Costa would climb up on the wall and sit and eat dates from his favorite tree.

These trees were about 25 years old and in their prime when we built the house. They were serviced annually by a special person who scaled the trees and kept them trim and neat. Each spring the tree-man trimmed and hand-pollinated them with supplies brought along with him. In the fall, late September or early October, the dates would ripen, the tree man collected them, and they were sold. This was done on a contract basis. We took as many as we wanted for our use. One day Costa asked me about making a date pie. Knowing nothing about making a date pie, I simply made a regular pudding and added chopped dates to the filling. He thought it was wonderful.

Penny

By late summer we began to prepare for the arrival of our second child. Costa wanted my mother to be in Baghdad for the expected birth in early October. Mother arrived in mid-September. The weather was still very hot, but within a few weeks it was cooler. Our daughter, Penelope (Penny) was born on October 3, 1953. Penny was a colicky baby, so the first three months were not easy for any of us.

My mother-in-law, even though she was Armenian, always made a Thanksgiving dinner complete with turkey and all the trimmings. She did not make bread stuffing, but prepared a beautiful rice stuffing with

75

nuts, raisins, pistachios, and spices. She was an excellent cook, and Thanksgiving being my husband's favorite holiday, she wished to please him.

The year that Penny was born, Costa's mother was not in Baghdad. We planned our Thanksgiving with my mother and some good friends, seven in all for dinner. I was going to prepare the dinner.

There was no such thing as a frozen or dressed turkey to buy in Baghdad, so I asked Costa, "What shall we do?" He told me he would find a turkey. The next thing I knew, there appeared this scrawny, cackling bird outside our kitchen door.

"What am I supposed to do with that?" I said. "I don't know how to kill or dress it!"

Costa said, "Don't worry, Sahib will take care of it."

We kept the turkey out in the back garden and fed it for a few days until the time came to slaughter it. When the time did come, Sahib asked me for some brandy or cognac. At first I believed he wanted to drink it, but instead he took a bit of cognac in a small glass and poured it down the throat of the turkey.

"Why did you do that?" I asked.

"To relax the turkey," he said.

So the turkey got relaxed, and next his head was chopped off. Then he was dunked in hot water for de-feathering. Once plucked and somewhat cleaned up, I took charge.

When we married, I knew nothing of cooking, so early on I had ordered a *Better Homes and Gardens Cook Book* from the States. (To this day, this is my favorite cookbook, even though I have a collection of dozens more.) For years it was the only cookbook I owned. Mother was there to help me; however, she wasn't particularly interested in involving herself in Baghdad culinary delights. She did help by answering my questions while I was working on dinner. That turkey was the scrawniest bird you have ever seen. The legs were long, very long. The turkey was barely enough for the seven of us even with the vegetables and side dishes that went with the meal. I made a pumpkin pie for dessert from a can of pumpkin Costa had found somewhere in the marketplace.

Mother remained through Thanksgiving, then returned to the States in early December. By Christmastime Penny was getting through her colic and began to thrive. All of us were much happier.

Food shopping in Baghdad was totally different from anything I'd seen anywhere else. The market was an open corridor lined with individual little shops. One shop would have meat, another would have fresh fish from the Tigris River. The vegetable and fruit shops in season were plentiful. There was a shop with tinned or preserved goods, usually from England or somewhere in Europe, but food was mostly local. Mayonnaise was not to be had. There was a salad cream that came from England with the consistency of little more than fresh cream. I disliked it intensely and learned to make my own mayonnaise, with egg yolks and oil. It was tricky, and if one didn't get it just right, it would curdle. Once a friend brought me a jar of American-style mayonnaise from Beirut, and oh, what a joy! I assigned it to the rationing section, doling it out very sparingly, and when doing so, stretched it a bit with milk or cream. Not only did I receive from my friend a jar of mayonnaise, but a roll of wax paper! Another treasure. I used, washed—carefully of course—dried, folded, and reused each piece again and again, as long as possible.

And that wasn't all. Once an Attaché Office friend brought us a can of Crisco from either Beirut or Bahrain, where they often traveled, bringing back scarce or unavailable items. Our good luck from one of their trips was the Crisco. Another treasure! It was relegated to the pie-making section in my kitchen and was also carefully rationed.

We quickly became very good at recycling scarce items in Baghdad. When there was a wedding reception among the Embassy family or at the Alwiyah Club, we used the decorations from a previous wedding. White crepe wedding bells that opened up needed to be carefully folded and put away for the next wedding. Our wedding was no different. Decorations had been used, more than once or twice before us, and who knows how many times after us. The word was easily passed along as to who had most recently used the wedding decorations, and where they could be found.

Gift wrapping paper wasn't to be had in Baghdad, so whatever came my way had already been used perhaps three or more times. Gifts were opened up *very* carefully, and the paper was ironed, saved, and passed on again along with the ribbon (if any) that had come with it. There was no Scotch tape either. The wrapping paper was glued together with egg whites or any other sort of glue at the seams. We could find glue, but no Scotch tape. To this day, I open up presents most carefully; I cannot just rip the paper off. My daughter, Penny, sometimes teases me. At a wedding shower she once said, "We all must be very careful with this paper because Mommy is going to take it home and iron it."

In earlier days I had once I found a tin of coconut in the market or received it as a gift and decided to make a coconut pie. We were having the Gleasons from the Attaché Office, the Kerins and two Marine guards from the Embassy. With that small of a dinner party it was foolish to have three different pies! But here I was with an apple, chocolate, and a coconut pie. When taking the coconut pie out of the oven of the kerosene stove, it somehow got turned upside down and ended up on the kitchen floor. There were still two other pies, but I was broken hearted—well almost—to lose my coconut pie, and I cried. But shortly the Kerins arrived, and Ruth assured me that two pies were more than enough for the eight of us. Of course she was right.

Furniture and clothing were passed around. When Embassy assignments were over and people were preparing to leave their posts, they sold their belongings and of course, much of their clothing. We bought our first kerosene stove, living room as well as bedroom furniture—all second hand. And I bought a black and gray tweed suit from Ginny Murphy. After wearing it for almost two years, Costa finally said to me, "Don't you have anything else to wear?" I loved that second-hand suit.

Before we built our home, we had cooked on the three-burner kerosene stove. This stove had an oven that was placed over two of the burners, so if one was baking, there was only one burner free. Because of this, most baking was done early in the day, so that all the burners were available for cooking a large meal. We had a French friend who gave a beautiful dinner party weekly. She did all the cooking herself, even though she had maids. Madame Michon had only a two-burner stove, like most everyone else. Once when in her kitchen, I discovered that she had three and even four pots stacked on top of each other over each burner to keep warm! Yet, she was able to turn out delicious French food, set a lovely table, and always entertained as an excellent hostess.

Shooting was a very big in Iraq, and Costa was an avid sportsman. However, over the past year or more, with building the house, a new baby, and my mother's extended visit, there had been few opportunities for him to exercise his passion. He loved to shoot wild boar, gazelle, partridge, sand grouse, geese and ducks. He was a great hunter; only he called it shooting. "The English go hunting," Costa would say, "I go shooting." He was a fantastic shot, never, ever missed. They didn't come any better! Once when I asked him, "Who is the best shot in Iraq?" His answer to me was, "Yours truly." This was an exceptional answer, because Costa was never a braggart or one to boast.

In late fall, when the partridge hunting season was ending, the goose season was beginning. July and August were Sand grouse season. Sand grouse are edible, but not the best—the flesh is tough, dark, stringy, and dry.

Russian geese passed over Iraq on their flights to Africa for the winter. This flyover took them by way of the Tigris, Euphrates, and/or the Diyala Rivers which ran through Iraq from the north to the south. In another time, Iraq had been termed the bread basket of the Middle East. Unfortunately, this is no longer the case. The "Land Between the Rivers" had once produced and exported great quantities of both wheat and barley as well as onions; thus these lands were a perfect haven for the birds.

Costa could now for the next few months resume shooting. He liked to go out on Fridays and Sundays with his favorite shooting companions, Vincent Asfar and Ralph Haddad, and he always returned with a great take, sometimes as many as 50 or 60 partridges or 15 to 20 geese. Lest I forget, ducks (both Mallard and Teal) were favored targets for him, and he might bring home 20 or more in a day. By the time shooting season was over, our large freezer was filled to capacity with game birds, as well as the freezers of friends and neighbors.

I was busy with our new home and Penny. Even though we had a cook and a nanny, there was much to be done. I supervised Penny's care, taught the cook the ways of the electric stove, as well as learned myself. There was need to clean, caress, humor and pet this special piece of equipment. With the able assistance of my *Better Homes and Gardens Cook Book*, I set out to bake every pie recipe in it. Costa's favorite was apple. First came apple, then a different one, then again apple, next another one, then apple again, and so on through the book.

Spring and summer came and went. The flowers in the garden flourished, becoming more lovely each day, and the lawn was a lovely carpet of green. Penny was doing very well and growing into a beautiful little girl with black curly hair. When the nanny took her for an outing, people would stop them and comment, "What a beautiful little girl."

Pierre Michon, whose mother could create a feast on a two-burner kerosene stove, and Barbara, an American girl who was employed at the Embassy as a Point Four employee were great friends of ours. Barbara and Pierre married in December of 1953, when Penny was just a baby. They had two girls right away, and then ten years later, they had two more girls. When the children were small, we would go to each other's houses for dinner and have such a lovely evening, we stayed the night. They would do the same at our house.

In September of 1954, Barbara and I decided to take a two-week trip to Beirut. We stayed at the old Bassoul Hotel near the Sea. The Bassoul was located almost exactly where the present-day Phoenicia Hotel now stands. This is also at the same area where the Old Lucullus restaurant was located. We shopped at Bab Edriss, Souk Tawili, and the Souk Jamil. We ate croissants until they came out our ears and

81

enjoyed all of the Lebanese delicacies, as well as many visits with friends. The weather was beautiful—as it always is in September.

My desire to see the world was not confined to the Middle East. So the following year, in early September 1955, Costa and I left Baghdad for a month's tour in Europe. While we were away, Penny remained at home with a friend's mother who was like a grandmother to her.

The trip, for me anyway, was all new territory and very exciting. Our first stop was Amsterdam. We spent six days visiting all the museums and admiring the many masterpieces of famous Dutch masters. We also had great fun floating along the canals.

From Amsterdam, we went on to Brussels where we again enjoyed the museums, the food, and the beautiful architecture of that lovely city. Then, too, we took a day trip to Liege for a visit with one of Costa's principals, an arms manufacturer by the name of Fabrique Nacionale. The Export Manager and his wife graciously invited us for lunch in their home. It was delightful.

Next came Zurich—just waiting for us! We spent eight beautiful days visiting friends, touring and shopping. I loved Switzerland. We stayed at the Hotel Baur au Lac on Lake Zurich. Marvelous shopping, marvelous food, marvelous time. It was great to again visit with Florence Neverman, former secretary to Ambassador Crocker in Baghdad, as well as Bill and Hillary Becket. Bill had also served at our Baghdad Embassy in the early '50s, and now both Bill and Florence were on assignments at our Zurich Embassy.

Our next stop was Rome and the surrounding area where we spent nine days. Rome was wonderful, partly because Costa had visited there at times in the past and knew his way around the city. He always loved Rome and was at his happiest when there. We enjoyed and experienced the bountiful sights and scenes of that Eternal City. The food was fantastic, especially Alfredo's. The weather was balmy and beautiful.

For side trips we visited Pompeii, Naples, and lovely Sorrento and Capri. From Rome, it was back to Beirut where we spent two days before returning to Baghdad and home to Penny. We were cultured and experienced world travelers! At least so we imagined.

During the winter of 1955-56, it was decided that we would travel to the States the coming summer. We had not been there since 1952. The plan was that I would go ahead with Penny in June. Costa would follow in August, and we would spend three or four weeks together before returning to Baghdad, either late September or October.

It was early June of 1956. As planned, Penny and I left Baghdad on the Nairn Bus for the 20-hour trip across the desert to Beirut. Nairn was a bus company owned and operated by Norman Nairn and headquartered in Beirut with scheduled daily bus service between Beirut and Baghdad. (If I recall properly, there was also service to and from Teheran.) There was a good enough road through Jordan and Syria, but for short cuts, Nairn traveled in what was simply a track across the desert. The desert track reduced the mileage by about 90-100 miles which considerably shortened the distance. As a rule, only heavy vehicles used this mile-saving route. We took the desert route—part of the way anyhow. Some people even said there would be robbers and thieves out there, but we never saw a single one!

In Beirut Penny and I stayed at the still-popular Bristol Hotel. It was my choice as Costa and I had spent two weeks there when we married in 1951, newly opened that year.

On the third day in Beirut we boarded the *Exeter* bound for New York. It was the one of the new Four Aces: the *Exeter*, the *Excambion*, the *Exochorda*, and the *Excalibur* owned by American Export Lines. Just before the Great Depression, American Export Lines built the original Four Aces and had them in service offering cruises for up to 40 days to the Mediterranean from the U.S. During World War II the vessels were taken over by the U.S. Army. Three were lost to enemy action, and the forth was converted to a military transport. After the war, American Export Lines purchased four attack transports, refitted them as passenger liners, and renamed them after the original Four Aces. They were sister ships of the *Independence* and the *Constitution* also owned by American Export Lines. These beautiful Four Aces, as well as their sister ships, became accidents of unsung history in the 1960s.

The Four Aces were used exclusively for travel between New York and the Mediterranean. Each ship carried 124 first-class-only passengers. Stops were made at Alexandria, Piraeus, Naples, Genoa, Barcelona, through Gibraltar, past the Canary Islands, then across to New York. The trip lasted 19 days.

From New York, we traveled by train to Chicago where my mother was living at the time. Within a few days, Mother, Penny and I took another train to Lansing, Michigan to collect a new two-toned green Oldsmobile from the General Motors factory. Costa had ordered the car through G.M. in Baghdad for my use while in the States. At the end of our stay, the car would be shipped to Baghdad.

We returned to Chicago with the new car, where we remained a few weeks before driving to our home in Kentucky in mid-July.

The plan for Costa to follow me to the States in August never materialized. There was a growing unrest in the Middle East. Advocates of Arab nationalism and opposition to Western political involvement in the Arab world was on the rise. Feisal II had come of age three years earlier and was crowned the third king of Iraq ending the rule led by his uncle the Regent. There was opposition in the country to the Baghdad Pact created in 1955, a U.S. brainchild, with Turkey, Iraq, Great Britain, Pakistan and Iran. Its goal was to prevent communist incursions (nonsense!) as well as to foster peace in the Middle East, but it was not popular with everyone. The political situation in Iraq was deteriorating, and there were uprisings in Najaf and Hayy.

Also, there was unrest in Egypt. For more than a year Gamal Abdul Nasser had been importing arms from the Soviet Bloc. The escalation continued, when in July, 1956, with the Egyptian blockade of the Tiran Straits and the nationalization of the Suez Canal, hostilities began. This was labeled *the Suez Crisis*. The United States withdrew from the building of the Aswan Dam which was later completed by Russia. In response, Israel in coordination with Britain and France attacked Egypt. There was talk of another world war. The crisis lasted through October of that year, then it was laid to rest—but of course only temporarily.

Penny and I were still in the States with Mother. By September, we had driven back to Chicago from Kentucky, and later that month, we drove on to New York. For a week we remained there, Mother having returned to Kentucky.

In the meantime I made arrangements to ship the car to Beirut and on to Baghdad. It was early October, when Penny and I embarked onto the *Andrew Jackson*, a cargo ship bound for Beirut. We were only 13 passengers, and all became good friends. We spent a most enjoyable time together on the ship. There were no ports of call on this journey, and the crew had nothing to do while at sea. I did learn to play Blackjack, which I've long since forgotten.

Penny was almost three years old. She had a grand time, but I kept losing her on the ship. Once I found her in the captain's cabin playing with the water in his sink. Another time I lost her, and she was sitting up on a crate with the sailors on the cargo deck. They were all gathered around talking and entertaining her or perhaps the other way around.

At times, it was a rough journey; Penny and I both became seasick for a few days. Once an engine went out, and we were floating out in the ocean for two or three days before it was repaired. Another time, the second officer became ill, and the Coast Guard was called to come along side of us; he was transferred to their ship, getting him to shore faster. The food was not fancy, but delicious and more than adequate. The trip was a long one, being on the water 23 days with no ports of call.

After arriving in Beirut and staying overnight at the Bristol, we then climbed again onto the Nairn Bus, and onwards to Baghdad.

That winter we did lots of entertaining, dinner parties usually, serving partridge as a main course, and Costa continued to keep our freezer well stocked. The menu varied little other than a different pie for dessert. I learned which day George, the number one houseboy at the Embassy, had off and engaged him to serve dinner. Our guests were not only delightful, but were delighted—with the partridge dinners anyway.

Stephanie Christine

You may give them your love but not your thoughts,
For they have their own thoughts.

Kahlil Gibran

The opposition against Feisal II began to heat up in February, 1957. The Front of National Union was established, bringing together the National Democrats, Independents, Communists, and the Ba'ath Party. An identical process ensued within the Iraqi officer corps, with the formation of the Supreme Committee of Free Officers. Feisal's government endeavored to preserve the military's loyalty through generous benefits, but this proved increasingly ineffective as more and more officers came to sympathize with the nascent anti-monarchist movement.

At the time, I did not know all of this but was well aware there were factions that were unhappy with the present government. The United States had made a treaty with Iraq in 1956 and sent in a number of military officers along with equipment for the purpose of training and assisting the Iraqi army. They were called the MAAG (Military Assistance Army Group.)

Costa had always been in close contact and on excellent terms with the Baghdad police department. We knew there was unrest in the country; Nuri al-Said, the strong man, was intensely disliked by a number of factions. Costa read the Arabic newspapers daily and thoroughly. He was perfectly aware of the turmoil that was going on. It was a festering sore throughout the years that the Monarchy had been created by the Western Powers, especially the British, for their benefit, and a pittance of benefit for the country itself.

In the early spring of 1957, we attended the Red Crescent Ball (Red Crescent is the equivalent of our Red Cross) that was presided over by the young King Feisal II. I remember he sat up high waving and smiling to the crowds. He appeared to be a likable and pleasant young man.

This was not our first encounter with King Feisal. Prior to the ball, on a particular morning in the mid-1950s, two high-up officials of the Security Department paid a visit to Costa in his office. The purpose of the visit was to summon Costa to the Palace. King Feisal, being an avid gun collector and perhaps a huntsman, was desirous of a particular shotgun. He needed Costa's advice. I believe the appointment was set for that very afternoon. Costa came home, changed into a suit and tie, and set off for the Palace. As he later related to me, the visit went very well. Feisal was gracious, and I expect Costa was no less. They drank tea together, and the King chose the shotgun of his liking from brochures. Costa returned to his office with a gun order for His Highness.

The shotgun was specially manufactured for the King, shipped to Costa for inspection, then subsequently delivered to King Feisal, who was extremely pleased and grateful to the most well-known and knowledgeable sporting arms dealer in the Middle East.

The Red Crescent Ball was elegant, and we looked forward to attending again the following year. In early 1958, I fell in love with and purchased a beautiful white lace gown with cap sleeves and a hooped skirt in anticipation of the next Red Crescent Ball, scheduled for April. At the time, I had no way of knowing there would be no Ball that year. I would never wear this lovely white dress. Through the years I carried it with me from Baghdad, to Athens, to Beirut twice, but there was never an occasion to wear it. Finally I gave it away, unworn.

In May of 1957, when I was expecting our third child, Costa's pointer Sallie gave birth to 14 puppies, and they all lived! The exhausted mother was unable to keep that many puppies fed, so I pulled out the baby bottles and filled them with milk. Twice daily, I prepared two boxes, putting all the puppies in one of them. Sitting on a stool by the kitchen door, each puppy was fed, one by one, then moved to the second box on the other side. I did this for six weeks. They all survived and were given to good homes.

Stephanie Christine arrived on July 18, 1957. There was a doctor and midwife in attendance. Though unheard of in those days, Costa was present at her birth. After a pleasant five-day stay in the hospital with many flowers and visitors, I returned home with our new daughter. Upon arrival at our front gate, I was greeted by our gardener, Sahib, with a young sheep in tow, holding a heavy machete-like knife. The moment I stepped from the car with the baby, the throat of the sheep was sliced and blood poured directly into my path. I was obliged to step over it. All this for good luck.

Life was comfortable and good. Throughout our years in Baghdad, I always felt we were a part of the Embassy family.

Up until July of 1958, all went along smoothly and uneventful for our family. Penny was ready to begin Kindergarten with the Sisters at Bab al-Shargi in the fall, and we were settled at home. All was well— we believed or wanted to believe. However, on the 14th day of that month everything changed for us forever. That was when our lives fell apart for years to come, as well as for thousands and thousands of other people.

In the wee hours of that morning, July 14thand Bastille Day in France, we were awakened by gunfire. Costa identified it immediately as heavy arms, saying, "This is not good." We did not sleep further, As soon as daylight broke, he took a scouting trip out and about. He discovered the palace had been assaulted. There was big trouble. No details yet, but we soon learned it was a violent overthrow—truly violent—of the government.

Earlier in the summer, King Hussein of Jordan asked for Iraqi military assistance during the escalating Lebanon crisis. Units of the Iraqi army under the command of Abdul Karim Kassem, supposedly en route to Jordan, chose to march on Baghdad instead, where they mounted a coup d'état. Feisal II, after being confronted, ordered the royal guard to offer no resistance. Feisal himself surrendered to the insurgents. About 8 a.m., the captain leading the revolutionary assault group at the palace, ordered the King, Crown Prince Abd al-Ilah; Princess Hiyam (Abd al-Ilah's wife); Princes Nafeesa (Abd al-Ilah's mother): Princess Abadiya (Feisal's aunt) and several servants to gather in the palace courtyard. Here, they were told to turn towards the wall. They were immediately shot by their captors. Feisal, who had not died during the initial fusillade, was transported to a hospital, but died en route. Feisal was buried in the Royal Cemetery and allowed to rest in peace. Princess Hiyam survived her injuries, caused during the massacre and later was able to escape the country. The coup was the brainchild of Abdul Karim Kassem and Abdul Salam Aref. Within the year both men died violent deaths.

Our airline tickets had been bought and plans had been laid to leave for Greece on July 16th to spend at least a month on Chios, our island. Of course we immediately understood that we would not be traveling anywhere—not yet!

The following day, July 15th, Nuri Pasha al-Said (the Iraqi politician who served seven terms as Prime Minister of Iraq under the Hashemite monarchy rule) was gunned down by tanks a few meters from Costa's office. Nuri Pasha had tried to leave the country disguised as a woman but did not escape. He was buried the same day, but an angry mob disinterred the corpse and dragged it through the streets of

Baghdad, where it was hung up, mutilated, and burned. Costa closed his office and came home. He was greatly shaken by this.

The next nine months were difficult for us. The army was everywhere, and our home was under constant surveillance. By Christmas, Costa would be arrested and detained three different times. I continued driving alone but only as necessary. Socializing was at a bare minimum. No one knew what would happen next. Thousands of people, including many of our Iraqi friends, were in jail.

Costa's first arrest took place in early August. It happened on a Sunday evening at around 8 p.m. There was a knock on our front door. He opened the door to face 18 soldiers. About half of them walked in. Uninvited, I might add. They searched the house and surroundings from one end to the other. We had had a large cocktail party a few days before this intrusion. The American Ambassador, Waldemar Gallman, and a number of government dignitaries had attended. The soldiers found the guest list and took it along with them. Then one of them announced that Costa was under arrest and would be taken away. He was escorted away from our home by the soldiers. Upon leaving, he told me, "I was born Iraqi and will be treated as one even though I am a U.S. citizen. Tell the Embassy not to interfere." He was taken away just after ten p.m.

I laid down to rest but never closed my eyes the entire night. At 6 a.m., I phoned Bruce Scrymjour, a CIA agent at his home and gave him our news. It was Monday morning. Later that morning, the U.S. Consul phoned to ask if she could come for a visit. I was of course pleased, and we set the time of her visit for the following day, Tuesday morning. She arrived at the appointed time. I thanked her for coming and offered her coffee and cookies. Within a few minutes of arriving, she asked if she could see Costa's U.S. passport. Of course I willingly obliged. After checking it for a moment, she said, "I will need to keep this." She dropped it into her handbag. I was aghast. She had come, not to console me, but to collect his passport. Shortly thereafter I learned that the Embassy was reporting that Costa had renounced his American citizenship. Nothing was further from the truth.

On the second day of his detainment, Costa was allowed to phone me. He had many influential friends in *the Security*, and with the help of some of them, he was released after six days.

Around this time an article was printed in the Baghdad paper about Costa. The first page of the article is missing, but he carried this part of the article around with him for years. This entire article is full of lies, misinterpretations, and turned confessions:

> **Testimony at the trial has indicated that the sabotage ring was created to blow up bridges and destroy roads in the event of a Soviet invasion or internal Communist coup. But the Government is trying to prove that the apparatus also plotted against Syria.**

These so called trials—nothing more than charades—began within a week after the coup. No one ever understood the meaning of apparatus, nor any plot against Syria, nor the blowing up of bridges or destroying roads.

> **Yesterday a witness testified that he was convinced that the funds for the apparatus had come from the United States**

Embassy. But he offered no facts to
sustain this conviction.

There was no truth to this whatsoever.

So far no testimony has been produced to
link Mr. Halkias directly with the sabotage
organization. Abdul Majid Bakeri, a retired
major, testified only that an accountant at
the Halkias store had paid "salaries" to a
number of members of sabotage cells.

This accountant was not trusted enough to pay anybody anything.
He would not have known enough to buy lunch for a stray cat.

Mr. Halkias was born in Baghdad of
Greek parents. He served in the United
States Navy during World War II. Returning
to Baghdad, he became a prosperous
retailer of household appliances and
sporting arms.
A few years ago he married an American
girl from Tennessee [They didn't even get this
right!] who was working as a secretary at the
United States Embassy. They have two
children.
A United States Embassy official said
tonight that no representations had been
made on behalf of Mr. Halkias. It was
reported that sometime after the July 14
revolution he had applied for Iraqi
citizenship.

Another lie!

In October, Costa was again arrested and taken into custody. This time, he was released after three days. His third and final arrest was on December 23rd. He was released into the hands of his good friend, General Sayem al-Askeri and brought home on Christmas Eve. Costa had become a man without a country.

By the first of the year, 1959, Costa told me that I must leave Baghdad with the girls. Naturally I protested. Of course to no avail. Finally the departure date was set for the day after Easter in April. At the beginning, we planned that I would return to the States, but as the time drew nearer, I decided I would rather go and wait for him in Greece. We had no way of knowing if this would mean weeks, months, or years. Maybe never! We also didn't know that this would be one of many times that Costa would be forced to abandon his work because of circumstances beyond his control.

The Hashemite Monarchy in Iraq was abolished after 37 years without consent from the people, and control over the country passed to a tripartite Sovereignty Council composed of representatives of Iraq's three major ethnic groups. A lengthy period of instability ensued, culminating in the ultimate triumph in 1968 of the Ba'ath Party which in turn led to the eventual coming to power of Saddam Hussein.

Since April, 1959, I have never been back to Baghdad, and I don't know if the house we built still stands. Surely, I couldn't find my way around the city, even if I tried. Such a mess has been made of it. It is a whole different world now. Thank you, George Bush! Had this man looked at a map of the Middle East, without the countries identified, he would have had no idea where Iraq is or was. Even when he was saying, "We are going to go and liberate these people," he did not even know who or where these people were! There was no way President Bush was going to liberate them. He may have sold the war to the American people as a war about weapons of mass destruction, but there was no way he could sell this war to the diverse nation of Iraq. One had to live there to understand it; even then we didn't always get it right.

The children and I left Baghdad the day after Easter of 1959, arriving in Athens for Holy Week of the Greek Orthodox Church. The Greek Orthodox follow the Julian calendar; whereas Catholics and Protestants use the Gregorian calendar. Costa stayed behind. His passport had been confiscated; he had no documents, nor permission to travel. Penny was five, and Stephanie was almost two years old.

This was my first trip to Greece, a country almost completely foreign to me. Costa had written to his sister, Maria, of our impending arrival date and asked her to reserve a hotel room for us, as well as meet us at the Ellinikon Airport (sometimes spelled Hellinikon.) My sister-in-law, Maria, did meet us at the airport and drove us to an old third-class, run-down hotel just off Omonia Square, a poorer section of Athens. We stayed there, most uncomfortably, for three weeks, after which time I did manage to rent a small and nicely furnished apartment in the Kolonaki area of the city. This did not particularly please Maria. She believed an apartment in Kolonaki to be far too elaborate or grand for the girls and me, and she had no problem continually reminding me of it. I tried not to let it bother me. I was never nervous about finances; Costa was always a good provider. He dealt with a money changer in Baghdad and easily transferred money to me in Athens. He was very good about making sure I had funds; he knew what I needed, and I was never at a loss.

In any case Kolonaki was, and still is, located in one of the better areas of the city. Shopping was nearby and downtown was within walking distance. We settled in at Anagnostopoulou 22. In June, Maria, as usual, began her *sea baths* routine as the Greeks describe it. She did, kindly and often, invite us to go along to the sea for the mornings. I was grateful as this was surely a diversion for us.

Except for Costa's sister and family, I was almost a total stranger in that city. There was a distant cousin by the name of Ioanna, a teacher by profession, to whom Costa had previously written. She gave me Greek lessons. I was pleased to know this kind woman, and to at least learn to communicate with the butcher, the green grocer, and the grocery store, or supermarket, as it was called.

Costa sold our home in Baghdad before leaving for Athens. He changed the money into gold ingots and sent them to me in the packing at the bottom of a refrigerator.

In June I had decided to go to Egypt, and booked passage for the girls and me on a ship bound for Alexandria for the first week of July. My good friends, Jean and Ralph Barrow from Baghdad, were now on assignment with the American Embassy in Cairo. They met us in Alexandria where we stayed overnight, before driving back to Cairo. For two weeks we remained in Cairo with the Barrows, doing all the touristy things that everyone does when visiting a new city.

By late July, I had returned to Athens with the girls. After leaving Baghdad, Costa and I wrote letters back and forth as best we could, but never spoke once on the phone during the entire time. Costa's two uncles, Mike and Demo, and his grandmother still lived on the property in Chios, but I had never been there. Finally Costa wrote, "Why don't you go to Chios? My uncles and YiaYiá (grandmother) would be very glad to have you and the girls." Thus, by mid-August we were on an overnight boat trip bound for Chios.

Chios in 1959

Chios

Through storms you reach them and from storms are free.
Afar descried, the foremost drear in hue,
But, nearer, green; and, on the marge, the sea
Makes thunder low and mist of rainbowed dew.

But, inland,—where the sleep that folds the hills
A dreamier sleep, the trance of God, instils,—
On uplands hazed, in wandering airs aswoon,
Slow-swaying palms salute love's cypress tree
Adown in vale where pebbly runlets croon
A song to lull all sorrow and all glee.

Sweet-fern and moss in many a glade are here,
Where, strown in flocks, what cheek-flushed myriads lie
Dimpling in dream, unconscious slumberers mere,
While billows endless round the beaches die.

Herman Melville, *The Enviable Isles*

99

The Greek island of Chios is the fifth largest of the Greek islands. It lies in the north Aegean Sea. Its neighbor to the north is Mytilini, Samos lies to the south, and 4.3 miles to the east is the village of Çeşme on the Anatolian (Turkish) coast, a 45-minute ferry ride from Chios Town across Chios Strait. By air, Athens is a 35-minutes plane ride; by ship it is eight to ten hours away.

Chios is a crescent or kidney-shaped island, approximately 31 miles in length and about 18 miles wide. The terrain is mountainous with a ridge of mountains running the length of the island. The average population is about 55,000, but during the summer this number swells to 60,000-70,000 due to the return of the ex-patriots with their families.

The island's climate is warm and moderate, categorized as temperate Mediterranean with modest variations. Average temperatures normally range from a summer high of 81°F to a winter low of 45-50°F in January and February. Below freezing can sometimes be encountered, and the winds can be icy and brutal. Rainfall is moderate and humidity may vary from 75% in winter to 60% in summer.

Chios is not particularly noted for its exports other than chewing gum. Mastic, or as the Greeks call it *mastica*, is used in the making of chewing gum. It is an aromatic resin produced by the mastic trees found in the southernmost part of the island in the seven mastic villages: Mesta, Pyrgi, Olympi, Kalamoti, Vessa, Lithi, and Elata. Together these villages have controlled the production of mastic gum in the region since the Roman period, 800 BCE to 500 CE. The resin is sun-dried into drops of hard brittle translucent resin known as the *tears of Chios*. When chewed the resin softens and becomes a bright white, opaque gum with a refreshing pine or cedar-like flavor.

It is sold in the villages, sometimes with sugar and flavorings added to it. The shops have it in big chunks. If you want local chewing gum, it can be cut off as small pieces and wrapped in newspaper for you.

Several other locally grown products include olives, figs, mandarins and cherries. Green olives are picked by hand. Workers must climb into the trees to gather them, and olive trees are very difficult to negotiate. Once the olives ripen in the fall, tarps are spread around the tree, the tree is shaken and the ripe olives drop onto the tarp.

Kardamyla, the area Costa's grandparents moved from, is located at the northeast sector of the island. South of Kardamyla, but still north of Chios Town lies the ancient village of Vrondados which claims to be the birthplace of Homer. The connection to the poet is supported by an archaeological site known traditionally as Teacher's Rock or Homer's Place. Our first trip to the beach with Uncle Mike was here. The castle in Chios Town was in ruins when I first saw it. No doubt it still is. We can only surmise, but most probably it was constructed closer to the 13th or 14th century. Most villages, built between the 14th and 16th centuries, have carefully designed layouts with fortified gates and narrow streets to protect against the once-frequent raids by marauding pirates.

The monastery of Nea Moni, built during the 11th century and declared a UNESCO World Heritage Site, was in 1952, due to a shortage of monks, converted to a convent.

The south coast of the island has two well-populated areas: the bay of Komi and the ancient village of Emporio, inhabited since 1800 BCE and the site of the black volcanic beach of Mavra Volia, believed to have been created by the explosion of Santorini Island in 1600 BCE. The stones in the courtyard of our home on Chios are from this beach at Komi.

The west coast between the deep natural harbor at the south and the town of Volissos in the north forms a crescent shaped series of almost uninhabited rocky bays. The nearest population centers are the two hillside villages of Lithi and Sidorounda.

On a side note: While visiting the beach just south of Volissos one summer, we almost lost John. He was about 20 years old. He took his windsurfer out on the water and because he was new at windsurfing, the current kept taking him further from the shore and out into the sea. Stephanie realized he was in trouble and was able to swim out and bring him back to the beach.

The people from Genoa, the Genovese, who were interested in profit rather than conquest controlled the trade ports and warehouses and in particular that of mastic. The island remained under Genovese control for two centuries. By 1566, when Genoa lost Chios to the Ottoman Empire, there were 12,000 Greeks and 2,500 Genovese living there. The island was invaded by Ottoman troops and absorbed into the Empire. During the Ottoman rule, the government and tax gathering remained in the hands of the Greeks. The Turkish garrison was small and inconspicuous.

In 1881, a tremendous earthquake damaged a large portion of the island's buildings and resulted in great loss of life. Reports of the time estimated between 5,500 to 10,000 fatalities.

In early 1882, when the Greek War of Independence broke out, Greeks from neighboring islands came to Chios to encourage the inhabitants to join the revolution against the Turks. The Ottomans responded with a massacre. Over 80% of the 120,000 Greek inhabitants of Chios were expelled, killed or enslaved. The news of this massacre sparked international outrage and increased support for the Greek cause.

During World War II, Chios was occupied by Nazi Germany, and as a result the inhabitants suffered extreme deprivation. This was true in all of Greece. The larger part of the Jewish community was hunted down, as in all Nazi territories, arrested, and transshipped to concentration camps for extermination. Some were even shot on the spot. Kondari beach is one example of this atrocity.

I can still see us that August morning arriving in Chios at about six a.m. Standing on the deck next to the disembarkment stairs with my two girls in hand, I spotted two older men looking up expectantly at us. One was dressed in suit, necktie, and hat; the other in suit, no tie, and a French beret. Uncles Mike and Demo had been well informed of our impending arrival along with all particulars. They were patiently awaiting the arrival of Costa's wife and children amongst the hordes of people gathered to collect their relatives.

After extensive greetings, we were loaded into a big old black Chrysler taxi, owned and driven by Yanni (John in English) who would be engaged as our driver for the entire stay. We were now on our way home which was little more than a mile from the port. Costa had well-prepared me. The house was very, very old, run-down, with dozens of nooks and crannies, but very clean. In the barn there lived a cow, a donkey, and a goat. Chickens were penned in another area of the garden, but two dogs and more than one cat had free rein of the place. Also there was a large pool or *sterna* with hundreds of happy goldfish. The water collected in the *sterna* was used to water the fruit trees. The seven-acre garden was host to predominantly orange and mandarin (tangerine) trees; there were also grapefruit, fig, and pomegranate trees. Naturally the girls were in seventh heaven.

I was escorted up to the third floor to settle into our rooms. While busying myself with unpacking, the girls explored the grounds. When finished, I went downstairs to the second floor where Uncle Mike was waiting for me in the salon. He told me to sit down on a chair and visit for a while. After a bit he excused himself and left to attend to something or another. He did not soon return, and as I was listening to much activity in the kitchen, I went to investigate. Shortly Uncle Mike was back inside to check on me, and much surprised to find me in the kitchen. He said, "Oh, but I thought you were a lady of the salon." He had been misinformed.

After the second day in Chios, we began to go regularly to the beach. Our first trip was to Homer's Place. I wore my bathing suit under a skirt and blouse as there were no bathing houses to change. While at the beach, I learned that the regulars had clever ways of dressing and undressing for a swim without exposing themselves.

The trips to the beach were pre-arranged. The old black Chrysler taxi would arrive at the appointed time with Yanni at the helm. The girls and I, chaperoned by Uncle Mike, were off to the beach. We had many choices. There was Kondari, Homer's Place, Los Bay at Vrondados, Agia Fotia, Karfas, Emborio, Komi and west across the mountains through Volissos, the beach at Agia Markella. Uncle Mike was always delighted to accompany us. He would dress up in his suit, tie, and hat to sit on a chair, not too far back from the water, while the girls and I played and swam. We'd often have lunch at the beach café. Always the same menu at *all* the cafés: Greek salad, fried potatoes and *kufta* (meatballs.)

The town, same name as the island, Chios had a population of perhaps 3,000 people, but Uncle Mike called it *the city*. "We will go to

the city and we will do shopping; we will do this and we will do that..."
He was in charge, always.

Sometimes in the evenings, especially on Saturdays, we would all dress up, go into town (usually on the bus as Yanni was with us only in daytime) and sit by the sea near the Port. We watched people dressed in their finery walking up and down along the *perivolta* while we nursed a lemonade until it was time to go back home again.

It was rather primitive living on Chios, but we ate well, and the girls were endlessly delighted. The calamari, fish, and eggplant were fresh and delicious. YiaYiá was no longer able to cook or do housework. Instead, the neighbor girl, Angeliki (Kiki),was responsible for cooking, cleaning, and laundry. Kiki had been working for the Halkias family for a number of years; she came every day at six in the morning and remained until about eight o'clock in the evening. Rather than sit and hold my hands in the salon or drawing room, I helped Kiki in the kitchen, but Kiki was the one to get the fire going. We cooked on charcoal.

Since Uncle Mike had lived in the States as a younger man, he had discovered that he loved apple pie. One day he asked me, "Do you know how to make an apple pie?"

"Of course," I said. "It is Costa's favorite pie." Since there was no oven in the house, I decided to make fried apple pies. My mother must have made a million (well, almost) fried apple pies in her day. I made up a crust and rolled it out with a wine bottle. Then used a coffee saucer to cut around, just like Mother did. For the filling, I stewed the apples, mashed them with a fork, then added a dab of butter, sugar, and cinnamon. (There was no ground cinnamon—only sticks that needed to be pulverized.) Making a small slit in each pie, I fried them in cooking oil, and while they were still warm, sprinkled sugar or dribbled honey over them. The Uncles thought they'd died and gone to heaven when they ate those fried apple pies.

The kitchen was quite large, but the entry was through an outside terrace. YiaYiá was a dear old lady, but by the time I came along she was very frail. She had a little daybed in the corner of the kitchen where she spent her days. She spoke no English so I communicated with her through the Uncles. I could understand a bit but wasn't good at speaking Greek, so I would say to Uncle Mike, "Tell YiaYiá this" or "Uncle Demo, tell YiaYiá that."

Uncle Mike never married, but he stayed in YiaYiá's bedroom with her. He had his bed and she had hers on the main floor. He slept in that bed in that same room from 1937 until she died in 1964. Our children very much loved Uncle Mike. He was so knowledgeable (self-taught), and the children delighted in sitting with him in the evenings. Uncle Mike became as a grandfather to all our children until his death in 1971.

After YiaYiá passed away in 1964, Uncle Demo married Kiki. They had two boys. Kiki was in her mid-30s and Demo was 64. Demo could not have married Kiki while his mother was still alive; she wouldn't have allowed it. YiaYiá was still slapping Demo's face now and then when he was well into his fifties.

August had passed; it was now September. Letters were few and far between. Communication was practically non-existent in and out of Baghdad. Contact was limited. There was no phone service from our house in Chios to anywhere. Since we had no phone, the only way to call Marie or anyone, was to go to the post office in town, make a reservation to place a call, then sit and wait. Sometimes the call would go through, usually it didn't. In the more than five months since leaving Baghdad, Costa and I had not spoken once. My sister-in-law Maria, however, had heard by letter from Costa that he was planning to leave Baghdad for Greece in September. Maria wrote to us in Chios with the news. A date had been set. Costa would transit Athens, take the ship and arrive in Chios the morning of September 18th. There was not yet air service from Athens; it would not begin until the early 1970s.

As Costa transited Beirut and boarded the flight to Athens, he reached his seat to find Joe Sheridan in the next seat. This was the same Joe Sheridan he had spent three months with on a ship traveling to the States in 1940. Though they had not seen each other for 19 years. They recognized each other immediately and were delighted to become reacquainted. This happenstance turned out to be the beginning of a great friendship between our two families. Both Joe and his wife Ellie have since passed away.

Costa was traveling on a *Laisse Passé,* a document he had managed to obtain through the good graces of his Security Department friends. With his arrival, we all were overjoyed to have him back with us again, alive and well.

Before his departure from Baghdad, Costa had sold our house with furniture. Only the carpets (Persian rugs) had been shipped to me in Athens. He left his office and all the merchandise for the business in the hands of people he trusted, and they promptly proceeded to dispose of and steal the *entire lot.*

Earlier in the summer I had registered Penny to begin first grade at the American Community School. By the end of September we returned to Athens as school was beginning the first week of October. Stephanie was still too young, just a bit over two years old.

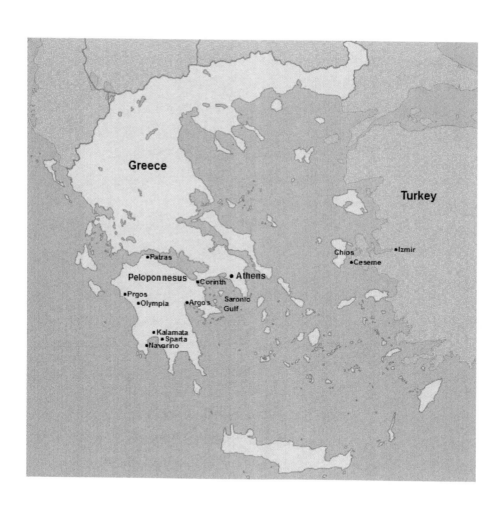

Athens (1959-1960)

With Penny starting school, we spent the winter in Athens. Shortly before Christmas, Costa's American passport was reinstated. After all, he was a Navy Veteran, had well served in other areas of the U.S. Government service, and over and above all, he had *certainly not* renounced his American citizenship.

However, by the time spring came and the weather had warmed, we began taking trips around the country—usually day trips. We did make a three-day trip through the Peloponnesus. Mostly over and through mountainous terrain, the roads were narrow and poorly maintained. The sojourn took us to Corinth, Argos, Sparta, Kalamata, Pelos (Navarino) Pyrgos, then north to Olympia. Driving further north we came to Patras, the principal port of Greece, on the west coast of the country. Afterwards we turned southeast to return through Corinth to Athens. The history of this region is most interesting and what a worthwhile experience it was to visit all these places!

Corinth Canal

When St. Paul arrived in 51 CE, the Corinth he saw was little more than 100 years old, but five times as large as Athens and the capital of the province. Ancient Corinth, the original Corinth, founded in the tenth century BCE, had been the richest port and the largest city in Ancient Greece. Strategically located guarding the narrow isthmus that connects the Peloponnesus to the mainland, it was a powerful commercial center near two seaports only four miles apart. The Western Harbor in the Corinthian Gulf was the trading port to Italy and Sicily. The eastern harbor, in the Saronic Gulf, was the port for the eastern Mediterranean countries. In 1893 the Corinth Canal was completed, and it connects the two gulfs, but because of its narrowness and steep walls that require periodic repair (no locks are employed), the canal is mainly used for tourist traffic.

Sparta, also known as Lacedaemon, was one of the key city-states of Ancient Greece located in the Laconia region, in the Peloponnesus, on the bank of the Eurotas River. Although it has been in existence since the tenth century BCE, Sparta became a truly dominant force in about 650 BCE. The city gained a reputation as a military power, and Spartan warriors were thought to be the best ground troops in all of Ancient Greece. In 480 BCE, King Leonidas of Sparta led a small army of 300 Spartan warriors against the Persians and killed many of them before the Spartans were defeated. This is known as the Battle of Thermopylae. During the series of wars between Greece and Persia (known as the Greco-Persian Wars), Sparta was in command of the entire Greek army. During the Peloponnesian War, however, Sparta and Athens fought against each other.

At all times, two kings ruled Sparta. One was to come from the Agiad family and the other from the Eurypontid family. The inhabitants of Sparta were divided into different social groups. Spartanites were citizens of Sparta, and Mothakes were non-Spartan free men. Perikoi were freed slaves, and Helots were slaves from Messenia and Lakonia. Life in Sparta was focused on producing warriors and maintaining Sparta's military supremacy.

Shortly after birth, Spartan babies were bathed in wine and then presented to the Gerousia, the Spartan elders. Any weak or deformed babies were thrown off Mount Taygetos and killed. Spartan boys began their military training at the age of seven. They learned to fight, survive on barely enough food, and learned to read, write and dance. They became athletic, tough and fierce. Spartan girls were also educated, but they did not receive as much military training.

Spartan women were respected, well educated, and had more power and status than women living in the other Greek city-states. The adjective Spartan used today, means simple and frugal. It comes from the character of Spartans from Ancient Greece. Only Spartans who died in battle and Spartan women who died in childbirth were entitled to having their names engraved on their gravestones.

Modern-day Pelos (once known as Navarino) is located on the southwestern coast of the Peloponnesus and is where the Battle of Navarino was fought during the Greek War of Independence in 1821-1829.

This war began as a rebellion of the Greeks against the ruling Ottoman Empire. The Ottoman treatment of the Greeks aroused the anger of Russia who saw itself as a protector of the Ottoman Christians in the Balkans. Britain and France came under pressure to take action as public opinion in both nations heavily favored the Greeks, and their rebellion became a *cause célèbre*. The Ottomans moved in their main fleet from Alexandria (Egypt) and rendezvoused with other Ottoman forces at Navarino Bay.

On July 6, 1827, Britain, France, and Russia signed the Treaty of London which called upon the Ottomans to suspend hostilities and grant the Greeks autonomy within a month. The Ottomans did not comply. The allied fleet in the Mediterranean moved to engage the Ottoman ships. For four hours the two fleets battered each other. As the fighting died out, over three quarters of the Ottoman fleet had been sunk. The remainder was disabled or burning. The Battle of Navarino proved to be a one-sided victory for the allies.

A turning point in the war, the Ottoman troops returned to Egypt. In 1829, after eight years of fighting, the Ottomans capitulated, and Greece finally achieved its independence.

The Greeks invented athletic contests and held them in honor of their gods. The Isthmos (Greek for isthmus) games were staged every two years at the Isthmos of Corinth. The Pythian games took place every four years near Delphi. The most famous games were held at Olympia, which also took place every four years.

The ancient Olympics seem to have begun in the early 700s BCE in honor of Zeus. No women were allowed to watch the games. (I believe the participants performed nude.) Only Greek nationals were allowed to participate. One of the Wonders of the Ancient World was a statue of Zeus of Olympia made of gold and ivory by Phidias. (Phidias was not the architect of the Parthenon, but the artist who oversaw the construction of the Parthenon on the Athens Acropolis.) This statue of Zeus was placed inside a temple even though it was a towering 42 feet high.

What began as a one-day festival was expanded in 472 BCE to a five-day event. These early events included foot races, wrestling, boxing, discus throwing (ancient Greeks considered the rhythm and precision of an athlete throwing the discus, a circle-shaped stone or iron, bronze or lead, as important as his strength) and animal sacrifices to the gods. The first international Olympic Games, as we know them today, were held in Olympia in 1896.

By the early summer we had decided to leave Athens. Costa did not wish to remain in Greece; he wanted to open an import/export business in a Free Zone where he could trade freely. It didn't matter to me where we lived, so I encouraged him to choose a place, and that was where we would go. Initially Tangier, an international free city in northern Morocco, seemed a likely place to settle. Of course returning to Baghdad was out of the question. We made reservations to go to Tangier, but at the last minute we cancelled and went to Beirut instead. The King of Morocco had revoked the charter granting free trade, and it no longer made sense for Costa to try to do business there. Years later while on a cruise, we stopped and spent the day in Tangier, and it was a lovely place, but because of the trade issue, Costa decided that Beirut would be the better place to reestablish himself. In June of 1960, we boarded a ship bound for Beirut.

Part III

On the sixth day, God turned to the angels and said, "Today I am going to create a land called Lebanon. It will be a land of outstanding natural beauty. It shall have tall majestic mountains full of snow, beautiful sparkly rivers cutting through forests full of all kinds of trees, high cliffs overlooking sandy beaches with an abundance of sea life." God continued, "I shall make the land rich to make the inhabitants prosper. I shall call these inhabitants Lebanese, and they shall be known as the most friendly people on Earth."

"But Lord," asked the angels, "don't you think you are being too generous to these Lebanese? Isn't it unfair for the rest of the world?"

"Not really," replied God, "Just wait and see the neighbors I am going to give them."

Popular joke in Lebanon

Beirut (1960-1967)

Beirut has always been special to me. I have never forgotten my introduction to the city when I had been invited to go on a one-day shopping and sightseeing spree on the Embassy attaché plane my first summer in Baghdad. Of course Costa and I were married in Beirut that same year. Also, we had many Iraqi and Lebanese friends who had moved there from Baghdad following the 1958 coup d'état; so when Costa decided to start up a business in Beirut, I was very happy.

Costa needed and wanted to be back in the business world after having been unemployed, as well as unoccupied, for almost a year. Soon after our return to Beirut, he traveled to New York. There he teamed up with American Eastern Corporation which he had done business with for many years. The principal officer, Marcel Wagner, was originally from Alsace Lorraine, a north-easterly region in France. American Eastern was well known and represented throughout the Middle East—primarily in the shipping world. Mr. Wagner was most receptive to the idea of Costa becoming associated with his company; thus a new entity was born: America Near East Associates. This new company, of which I would become a part, would promote and represent various U.S. companies in the Arabian Gulf. Costa would become the backbone of this new company, and it would involve a great deal of traveling for him. By early fall, he had opened an office in Kuwait and linked up with a Kuwaiti sponsor.

We also established a small Beirut office that same year, in the name of J. Rudolph & Co. which operated for 47 years.

There was no American school in Kuwait, and as we wanted our children to attend the American Community School (ACS), it was necessary for our family to remain in Beirut.

Our first trip to Vienna took place in September 1960. First, we stopped over in Athens for a few days to visit with Costa's family. It was Wine Festival time, and a new experience for me even though I had been in Greece during the month of September before. Then we proceeded on to Vienna where we were to spend a delightful ten days.

Besides shopping, enjoying the wonderful food, and taking in the sights, Costa introduced me to the world of opera. He was always interested in and enjoyed classical music, having grown up surrounded by music. When our children were young, he loved to put classical music on, sometimes a bit loud, even early in the mornings. It wasn't that I didn't enjoy it, but it was not something I needed to hear when making sure the children were ready for school.

While in business school, my first exposure to classical music came when I was invited to attend a not-so-amateur production of *The Merry Widow* in Peoria. The second was *Swan Lake* in Denver, produced by Sadler's Wells, starring Margot Fonteyn. My roommate Angie and I purchased tickets for the cheapest seats; still we enjoyed one of the best. Somewhere along the way, I believe I did see Moira Shearer in *Red Shoes*.

At the Statz Opera, we delighted in the performances of *The Rosenkavalier* and *Aida*. Both performances were performed by outstanding and world-famous artists. Most exceptional was Leontyne Price who starred in the memorable role of *Aida,* composed by Giuseppe Verdi and opened in Cairo to great acclaim on December 24, 1871.[5]

---

[5]Two famous misconceptions: Italian composer Giuseppe Verdi composed Aida 1. for the opening of the Suez Canal. 2. for the inauguration of the Royal (Khedival) Opera House. Both wrong! Verdi rejected the offer: "I do not compose occasional pieces!"

Andreas Augustin *THE MENA HOUSE TREASURY*)

http://www.famoushotels.org/article/517

Katherine Constantine

You may house their bodies but not their souls,
For their souls dwell in the house of to-morrow,
Which you cannot visit, not even in your dreams.

Kahlil Gibran

In May of 1961, when I was expecting our third daughter, we made a two-week trip to the States. First, it was New York for business and where I had the opportunity to shop for some lovely maternity clothes. Next, we took a quick trip to Kentucky to visit Mother.

On September 26, 1961, Katherine Constantine was born. Costa had taken me to the Khaldi Hospital, where Dr. Alex was waiting for us. A few minutes before Katherine was delivered, Alex told Costa, "Wait outside. I will call you when it is time." When Alex went out to call Costa in, he was nowhere to be found. Later when he asked, "Costa, where were you?" He answered, "I went to the Mayflower [Hotel] to drink a beer."

When Katherine was a newborn, we called her Baby. Later she became Kathy, but soon, at four or five years old, we began calling her Katherine. I felt she had grown into her name.

I should have given all my children Constantine as a middle name because that was their father's name, but I didn't become aware of this until Katherine's birth. Penny's middle names are Anne Therese after an American nun whom I much admired, and Stephanie's is Christine after a dear friend who passed away shortly before Stephanie's birth. Costa didn't seem to mind that I didn't follow the tradition; otherwise, he would have told me so.

Our office hours were from 8:30 a.m. until 2 p.m. Sometimes I would go in on Saturdays, and often times the children would come along with me. At times, Costa would insist that I be in the office in the weekday afternoons, but I needed to be home. Sometimes he did not understand. He seemed to feel that servants could do everything. They couldn't. The children had homework and would sometimes get into disagreements. I needed to be nearby. There was a time Costa wanted us to engage a nanny from England; this was not to my liking. I did not need the responsibility of entertaining an English nanny in Beirut. Anyway, it was not common practice at that time.

These were not days I wish to relive. After rereading more than 300 letters which Costa had written to me in 1962, and another 300 some letters from me to him, only now have I come to realize that this year was probably one of the most difficult of our 54-year marriage.

Costa was extremely stressed in his effort to create a successful business. With headquarters in Kuwait, he needed to maintain an intensive traveling schedule throughout the Arabian Gulf, and he was obliged to spend much more time in the Gulf than in Beirut with his family.

The Baghdad business was slowly, but surely, being totally destroyed. This greatly distressed Costa and demanded much of his time and energy. The effort he put into trying to get it back on track was extremely heart rendering for him. A once-thriving 40 year-old business was being frittered away. He continued, however, to pour money into the dying Baghdad operation, but it was a bottomless pit. Besides, he was unhappy that I was living in Beirut; inherently he was suspicious as well as jealous by nature. There were people in Kuwait, friends of Costa's, who without a shadow of a doubt, would come to visit me in the Beirut office, then return to Kuwait to feed lies to my husband.

All these things lay heavy on his mind and made him miserable. I was the accused one and bore the brunt of his misery. At times he was like a yo-yo, up and down in his moods.

One of the letters I wrote to Mother, at this time of my life, survived. It paints a small picture of what life was like for our family during these days.

June 19, 1962
Dearest Mother,
I guess you are run ragged with all the work you have to do. Just as I thought—Ma and Pa just think it isn't necessary to get a woman to help out. Even if I were there, I'm afraid I wouldn't be much help to you with these three poor little helpless children I have. Sometimes I think if it weren't for them, I'd just throw in the sponge, leave everything and come home. I don't know how much longer I can stand up under the strain, and I don't mean the children, either. I thought for a few months it was over and done with, but now I see that it isn't. You say there is a way for everyone—maybe there is—but I often wonder where mine is.
Stephanie is fine now. I did not send her back to school after she was sick so now she is at home and plays outside most of each day.
Penny finished her examinations today and her school will be out on Saturday if she hasn't failed third grade. She has come awfully close to it, I know. She just will not study no matter how hard I get after her.

She pretends to study and will say she knows her lesson, I offer to help her and it's no use. She says she knows it, and then she doesn't know anything at all. She is not stupid, but is downright lazy and doesn't care a nickel's worth.

Katherine is sick with diarrhea today and I took her to the doctor. She is about to cut two upper teeth, so it is probably partly that, and she has no doubt picked up some dirt. She loves to crawl and sometimes we put her down on the carpet; she can go all over the place. So now she is on diluted milk only—no food—and medicine every six hours. Her little bottom is fire red and raw as can be. Poor little thing just cries and cries because it hurts her so much. Tomorrow I'll get some salve that I know is very good for rawness.

On Sunday night I had five little neighbor girls and with Penny and Stephanie, made seven, for pizza, salad, cupcakes and ice cream. You should have seen them—they ate like little pigs and had such a good time.

I guess I like being here in this apartment about as much or more than any place I've ever lived. The children have lots of playmates—something they never had before and we have awfully nice neighbors. Two of the women I am particularly fond of.

All of the children are about our children's ages. I feel lucky, as I've never had nice close neighbors before.

We go back and forth and have a nice time together.

This afternoon I phoned Costa. I had intended to go to Kuwait tomorrow for a few days but I called him to tell him the baby is sick and I can't leave her. Well he was as mad as an old wet hen and just carried and carried on, saying I didn't want to come and all kinds of silly things. If I'd take care of the children better then they wouldn't be sick, and I don't know what all.

When Stephanie got sick before, I had planned to go to Kuwait on the 30th and she got sick on the 29th. So this is my luck and he blames me for it or thinks I'm lying—maybe both I reckon.

Well I hate to write such things, but if I were there I'd tell you anyway so I guess it makes no difference.

If I could tear myself in four pieces, put one in the office, one at home here, one in Kuwait, and the fourth I would bring home to you. And the fourth piece and the second piece would be the biggest pieces.

So enough of my silliness and complaining for one night. I'd better get to bed as I have to get up at 12:30 to give the baby medicine.

With love from all of us. Jessie

In the latter part of 1962, I became ill with Hepatitis C. For a short time I improved, but it did not last. By early February 1963, we moved back to town, but I was unwell during the time of the move. Almost immediately, I suffered a relapse of the hepatitis virus. I spent three months in bed and was seriously ill. When Mother learned of my relapse, she booked a flight and immediately came to Beirut. Before she left Moline, her friends gave Mother a hard time. "Oh, Girlene how can you go? It's so dangerous over there."

"Oh, they've been fighting over there for 10,000 years." That was her attitude; she wasn't worried about *them*. She was worried about me.

Our doctor was also concerned; he was not sure I would survive. At his suggestion, Costa booked a space for me at a Kurhotel in Schruns, Austria for treatment.

Shruns

On May 31,1963, Costa and I flew to Zurich, then traveled on by taxi to the village of Schruns in western Austria, where I was immediately checked in at the Kurhotel. This facility was owned by Dr. Edwin Albrecht who was a close friend of Marcel Wagner. There, I would remain as a patient for six weeks. Costa did stay in Shruns with me for ten days, then returned to the Middle East.

The Kurhotel was located directly on the Montafon River, which runs through the village. This is the Montafon valley in the Voralberg Region of western Austria. The other nearest villages are Feldkirch and Bludenz, which lie east of Lake Constance.

Mother was with the children in Beirut while I was in Schruns. Penny was ten years old; Stephanie, six, and Katherine, two. We had two full-time maids and a driver. They spoke very little English, but the two older children spoke enough Arabic to help Mother. She was not alone.

```
Schruns
Noon, June 10, 1963
My Darling Costa,
    When I got up this morning and
looked around, seeing all your things
gone, I just felt like crying.
    I so hope the children are all
right, and that you will write and
tell me all about them, how they are
getting on and all. Also tell me what
Mother said about staying on til at
least 15th July and if you asked
Muntaha [our maid] about going to
Chios, or if anything new has been
decided.
    With all my love to you as always,
    Yours, Jessie
```

It was a beautiful facility, and the care was excellent. As young women often tend to do, I fell in love with my doctor! However, no one ever knew that other than myself.

```
Shruns
June 11, 1963
    Like a fool this morning, I began
crying on the phone, instead of having
my proper wits about me. I'm sorry,
but I couldn't help it.
```

It is rainy and dreary today—just like last Friday morning when you were on your way back to Geneva.

In two days—this morning—I have finished *To Kill a Mocking Bird* whereas it took me two weeks to read *Anna Karenina*. Now I begin *The Blue Nile.*

Last night I sat in the small room off the lobby a few minutes before dinner to read. Mrs. Martini came along and asked me if I was all right and how did I feel as you had left. I could only answer—lonely.

I wish with all my heart that you manage to sell the air conditioners and refrigerators quickly. Somehow can't we spend more than a week or ten days together next time?

Schruns
June 15, 1963
I have spent the past 48 hours in bed except getting up to eat here in the rooms. I went for glucose this morning. I had a lot of pain in my side and I thought I could see my eyes turning yellow again. So I lay in my bed and cried and cried. But this morning Dr. Romani said my eyes are the same. He checked my urine and blood test for the day before and said there is nothing to show that I should be sick again. I have been so frightened to fall in bed again.

I asked Dr. R. why I couldn't have glucose every day instead of every two days, but he said it's good for the liver, but the veins couldn't take it so well every day. I wish I could have it every day so that maybe I would get well more quickly.

As it looks like I will run out of something to read, I'll go through the *Agony and the Ecstasy* again.

Schruns
June 17, 1963
I thought it was done and decided that we would go to Chios, then you say in your letter that "Samia could look out nicely for the children." By her just <u>only possibly</u> being able to spend an hour or two with them <u>maybe</u> every second day is not my idea of somebody looking out for them. And besides that, I can't stay month after month without them. I should slowly but surely go mad. Last Christmas, in the dead of the winter, you wanted that we bundle them all up and go to Chios for Christmas. Now in the middle of the summer—when it's certainly the only sensible time to go to Chios and stay in the house in its present condition—you tell me it's not wise to go there. But you do not tell me why. I am not angry, Sweetheart, please believe me, but I just don't understand. They will have the time of their lives there—and I know Uncles too will help a lot to take care of them—you have said so yourself.

Schruns

June 18, 1963

Last night I finished a book on Kamal Ataturk. My goodness—what a tyrant this man was! Anyhow there was nothing else to read except begin *Michelangelo* again which I did. At noon, in the dining room, I saw Mr. Martini so I asked him for some books. By the time I finished lunch he was back with five. Not a single one I've ever heard of before—except a murder mystery by Agatha Christi. Well, whatever they may be, I shall read them.

Schruns

June 19, 1963

Just this minute, I have received a dozen beautiful yellow roses—and have learned they are from you. Thank you so very, very much my Darling.

The story about the warehouse with the hole in the wall is incredible. Is there nothing that that thief of a Levon would not stoop to do? What a low-down dirty man he is. When he was in Beirut and came to the office recently, I wonder what he was looking for and expected to get? All I can say is, that he was lucky that he didn't find me there. This whole Baghdad situation, Sayem included, seems so hopeless every time I think about it. It is for you to decide what to do with it, but I firmly believe that the sooner things can be straightened out to a reasonable degree, and then sold if possible, then the better off you will be. No matter what happens, I don't believe that it can ever be revived to any point where it can be really worthwhile—not while it is in the hands of such people as are now there. Forgive me if you think I speak too strongly—I am only thinking aloud.

Also there was a letter from Mother today. She said she must go by the end of the month. I will get a letter off to her tomorrow telling her that I must stay here until around the tenth, and that she must try to stay until that time.

Schruns
June 21, 1963
I have a new friend. She is a very old woman (70 maybe.) She sits in the place where that insipid looking Frenchman with the white crew cut used to sit. She is a Baroness from Vienna and has arthritis. I have been talking to her for about a week now and only today I found out who she is. Sister Emmi says she comes here every summer for two or three months.

Shortly after my arrival in Schruns, Costa shipped a car to me. I made little use of it, as I did not feel well enough even for the shortest drive out and around.

Shruns
June 22, 1963
I forgot to tell you, I bought myself a kilo of apples—16 shillings—

yesterday. At last I have put something in the little refrigerator, and my apples are handy and much cheaper.

When I went for my injection, I asked Dr. Romani if I could drive. He said, "Why do you ask me when you have been driving all the time." I told him only once or twice and that was ten days ago. But I have decided I will go out tomorrow a little and every day that I feel like it, now that the weather is much nicer too. It has been really warm today, but now it is clouded over and probably will rain tonight <u>again</u>.

Oh, you won't believe it, but I had an apricot tart with cream—real cream—for dessert at noon. They are beginning to slacken up a bit on the diet.

So far I have had nine infusions of glucose. Dr. Romani said today that four or five more and it should be enough.

Shruns

June 24, 1963

Now you will let me know on which flight you will be coming to Zurich on the 10th. I will meet you in Feldkirch on the first train coming from Zurich after your plane is due to arrive.

I am glad you talked to the children and they are fine. Of course I know they are all right and are being taken care of well enough, but I still can't keep wondering and thinking about them. And being here, I feel so awfully far away from you.

Shruns

June 25, 1963

As planned I went to Mrs. Albrecht
for tea. The most pleasant part was
meeting their 22-year-old daughter, a
very sweet girl who has come from
school in England. We had King
Feisal, Nuri Said, and Taksin Qadri
strictly ala carte. It has begun to
remind me of the chicken dinners we
used to have with Pierre and Barbara.

Their house is sort of a dismal,
depressing sort of place in an
attractive sort of way. They have
some Persian carpets scattered around,
odds and ends and what-nots of all
different sorts, and a couple of brass
trays. She pointed these out to me
and said she hoped they would make me
feel at home. Shortly before it was
time for me to leave—I stayed an hour—
a guest book was produced and I was
allowed to sign my name.

From the looks of things, I am
being given the standard treatment for
distinguished guests; and I would
venture to say that most distinguished
guest of the hotel—like Taksin Qadri
and Mrs. Wagner probably get invited
to dinner. All the same when they
come to Beirut—and they will—we shall
reciprocate as gracefully as possible.

Shruns

June 26, 1963

Tomorrow I must go for an x-ray to
Maria Rast. Sister Emmi will go with
me. We had a nice long talk this

morning while I took my glucose. I casually mentioned to her that it would be nice to have a girl from here to help in Beirut with the children, and I almost think she would like to go herself. She has a friend who went through nurse's training with her, who is now working for a family in Beirut, either English or American. I hope you don't think I'm crazy, but it would sure be nice to have someone like her around with the children. Of course I don't know what someone like her would expect for salary—it might be far too much.

Shruns
June 27, 1963
This morning at 8 I had an x-ray and then at 9 a second one, and finally my breakfast at 9:30. By that time I was quite hungry and thirsty; and now I've come from having another vitamin B shot. Maria Rast is a full-fledged hospital run by nuns. It seems that this was Dr. Albrecht's first establishment and the Kurhotel came afterward.

I had a letter from Mother and the children this morning. Also a nice picture of Baby. Even in this short time she has changed. She looks bigger and more grown-up. The children sent me their grades from school and they are nothing to brag about.

Shruns

June 27, 1963 afternoon

I took the car around 4 to the garage across the street from us and had it washed. They did a much better job than the station down the road, but it still isn't exceptionally clean.

Shruns

June 28, 1963

You tell me not to worry about petty things. It is not a petty thing, Darling, that for months on end, I am costing you such a lot of money for doctor and hospital bills and medicine and being of no help either to you and the children.

Mr. Wagner may very well be an old goat, but let it not worry you—his interest in my health and well-being is all indirect—I dare say it is all connected up with dollar signs. He knows very well that when a person is anxious or worried, that person cannot produce the way he would when he has peace of mind. Anyway, I will explain better to you what I mean when you get here. No, I shall write to him only when I have reason to; otherwise, why should I?

You are my husband, I love you, and nearly burst with pride for you and for what you are. You are the one for me to be proud of—not the other way around. Without you I am nothing—as I have told you many times before.

Shruns

June 29, 1963

I have received one dozen red and white roses this morning. Thank you my darling—they are very lovely and fresh.

Just now I have come from Dr. Romani (for the injection.) He said the x-rays showed my liver very nearly returned to normal, but for one year I must stay on a strict diet, which does not make me awfully happy.

Penny made Fs in History and Geography. I am tired of battling with the Italian school. If you want, we will go ahead and put her in the American Community School. You can look into it when you come through Beirut. And I know she is dying to go there—but if Penny goes, then Stephanie must also go.

Shruns

July 3, 1963

If I go to Beirut, I'm afraid to start doing too many things, then get sick again. Whereas if I am in Chios, I won't have anything to do, except that which I want to do in passing my time in reading and resting and sewing a little. And it would be just the same if I had Penny and Stephanie with me. They are big now and all they need, except you and me to love them, is their food prepared and a little washing of their clothes. They can make their own baths, dress and amuse themselves—that is if Mother will stay in Beirut with Baby, and she said she would stay as long as I am away.

Kiki and Uncles will be plenty of help for Penny and Stephanie. You can arrange when you are in Beirut for them to come—they are plenty big enough to make the trip alone, then we could meet them in Athens. Please think about this, Darling.

This is the last letter I am sending to Kuwait. Until after the weekend, I'll write you in Beirut then I won't write anymore after Monday or Tuesday.

P.S. Bring me some cigarettes if you want.

Shruns

July 4, 1963

Today I went to town and took the chair lift up the mountain. The air was wonderful with the smell of the wild flowers and the pine trees. Also, before we got very high, there were some farmers doing up their hay. I spent about an hour at the top.

I think Sister Emmi would like to come to Beirut but she isn't sure that would be the thing to do, that is, giving up her job here, leaving her brothers and sisters (her parents are both dead), etc. Anyway if she would accept to come, and it is a big IF, she would not do so right away, I'm sure.

Could you bring my old black swimming suit with the buckle in back? It is looser and more comfortable than

the other black one, and I can't bear
anything tight on my waist.

Shruns
July 5,1963
Since morning, it has looked like
rain—dreary outside. Even so, I drove
to Feldkirch before noon to learn the
place of the station and finally found
it after lots of winding and twisting
around. Although the weather wasn't
nice, I enjoyed the drive very much.
The car really is a dream—it is such
a pleasure to drive.

We had fish for lunch. They served
me a fish the likes I have never seen
before—had the girl set down a snake
in front of me, I would have felt no
different, as it was a grey and blue
spotted thing (it had been boiled.) I
got all nervous in myself and started
to cry. Isn't that silly now? But I
sent the fish back because I couldn't
eat it. so I ate my potatoes and salad
and that was that. My neighbor, the
Baroness said, "Why did you send the
fish away? It's the most expensive
kind of fish." I told her, "If it cost
a million dollars I wouldn't eat it."

She is Baroness Bolshenk and every
day she asked me how I pass my time.
She cannot possibly imagine what I
find to do all day—she is a funny
woman, but a bit nosy or should I say—
inquisitive. But she is old—80 years,
Sister Emmi told me.

Yesterday, again I mentioned to her
[Sister Emmi] about coming to Beirut.

She says, "But what about Dr. Albrecht?"
So I don't know, but she has been the
one really bright note in my stay here.

One more week and you will be here.
I'm so happy, so very happy! Kiss the
children and hug them one by one—
Penny, Stephanie, and Katherine—and
tell them I love them and miss them.
I hope I shall be seeing at least Penny
and Stephanie very soon.

Shruns
July 6, 1963
I feel better this week than I did
last. But sometimes I get depressed
and wonder when, or if ever, I shall
feel normal again, and be able to do
my duties toward you and the children.

Now my main thought is that you
will be here next Saturday, and I'm so
happy, and also if you will give me
Penny and Stephanie in Chios.

Shruns
July 8, 1963
Don't forget about Stephanie's
birthday. It's the 18th you know. I
thought she might enjoy having Joni
Goodridge spend the day with her. so
you and Mother should phone up Lois
and ask for Joni to come down on the
18th. This would be just as nice for
her as having a birthday party, and
not nearly as much trouble.

This is the last letter I'll write
to you as you won't receive this
before Thursday or Friday.

Two days later I met Costa at the train station in Feldkirch. The following day we began our drive back through Switzerland, spending the first night at Como on the Lake. The following day in the late afternoon, we reached Florence to spend the night. From Florence, we passed through Rome, arriving in Naples in the late afternoon. It is a 90-mile trip from Rome to Naples, and we drove it in one hour. At Naples, we took the drive along the Amalfi coast, which Jacqueline Kennedy made famous by vacationing there the previous summer. This drive is the most stunningly beautiful piece of scenery anyone would ever want to see. We stayed in Amalfi one night and the following morning left to drive across Italy, through the Apennine Mountains to Brindisi. There we boarded a ship with our car for a 24-hour trip to Patras in Greece where we disembarked and drove on to Athens.

All that fretting about not having the children with me in Chios must have paid off because Mother, as Costa had pre-arranged, and the three children were waiting for us at the Athens Hilton when we arrived from Patras. For three days we all stayed at the Hilton and sent Mother out sightseeing. She then left for the States, and Costa and I took the car and children on the ship to Chios. Costa remained only a few days, I believe. However, the children and I stayed on the Island for the next two months.

```
Chios
Jessie to Costa
July 27, 1963
    Yesterday we did a lot of running
about.  The car in the morning, then
to the sea after lunch and back to
```

141

town in the afternoon to have the car washed—it was covered with salt.

As you know from the telephone, the car arrived in very good order, not a scratch, and as you might imagine, it has created quite a sensation in town. How I wish you were here to see! It is really funny. It just barely passes through the gate coming into the house, and with lots and lots of see-sawing, I manage to turn it around.

The sea was wonderful yesterday—so warm and calm—I went in for the first time and enjoyed it.

We all went together, Demo, Kiki and her cousin (whom I will not accept to work after all) and the children. We enjoyed but I wished for you—as I do constantly anyway.

Tomorrow we are thinking to go to Homer's Place, on the other side of town—you remember. Uncles say the beach is very nice there.

The children are still very happy and busy, busy all the day long, and Katherine still hates her potty chair. She is still throwing her usual fits.

On your return to Kuwait, you must have had a million and half things to do. But I want you to know that for me, it was a wonderful twelve days we were able to spend together—the longest time we have been together since Christmas.

I wish you good luck in getting a big order quickly so that you can go ahead to the States and finish there

and be back with us as soon as
possible.

The refrigerator is working fine
and Monday we will use the washing
machine to do the big washing and see
how it works.

P.S. Katherine just christened her
pot!!

Chios
Jessie to Costa
July 31, 1963
For the past two days Baby has been
sick and I have been up most of the
last two nights with her and during
the day I cannot let her alone for a
minute. So this morning Uncle Mike
went with me to the doctor with her.
She has had fever and vomiting, but
I'm sure by tonight or tomorrow she is
going to be all right as I'm giving
her medicine now.

Kiki's cousin has been helping us
the last few days which has been a big
help. There is no end to the cooking
and washing and ironing. But I refuse
to tire myself and will take care of
Katherine most of all.

On Monday, Uncles started watering
the garden so they have been rather
busy. We had the big washing to do.
I prepared the uncles to show Kiki how
to use the washing machine but the
thing wouldn't work a lick so they had
to do the washing on their hands.

Also, Monday just before noon, the
relatives sent word that YiaYiá's
sister had died that morning and they

would bury her that afternoon. So
Uncles had to go. She was 97 years
old.

We had planned to go swimming
yesterday, but due to Katherine being
sick, I could not leave her. Any how
this afternoon, KiKi took Penny and
they all went to Kondari on the
donkey.

The night before last, an owl came
in through the window during the
night. It took me about 20 minutes
before I could get him out. Finally
I managed to knock him senseless with
a magazine and threw him out the
window. Then again last night the
same one, or another one came, but I
caught him at the window and beat him
until I was able to throw him down. I
don't know if they are dangerous or
not.

Penny and Stephanie are enjoying
themselves whole heartedly as you
might expect.

Chios
Jessie to Costa
August 3, 1963
You can imagine how detached and
out of touch I feel with your work and
everything you are doing. I so much
miss being able to help you. I am
glad you have sold all the radios and
that Victor at least managed to
dispose of six of the air
conditioners.

The new woman is working out well
enough—as long as she doesn't take

YiaYiá to heart, it will be all right. Poor YiaYiá is in a terrible state. I do believe that her mind is almost completely gone. She doesn't give anyone a minute's peace. Mostly, I am sorry for Uncles—they are nearly driven out of their minds at times. Two times she locked herself in her room and Uncle Mike had to take the ladder and climb through the window to open the door. This sort of thing is awfully hard on those who have to look after her.

I cut the children's hair this afternoon, about two or three inches. So now they are with pony tails again. I was getting a little sick of braids.

Chios
Jessie to Costa
August 5, 1963

We have tried again the washing machine today—it's of no use with the present transformer. The men that were here the other day say that they can make a bigger and more powerful transformer and then it should work. We will try it and if it still doesn't work, I will be obliged to give it up, I'm afraid.

I intend to take Penny and Stephanie to the beach again this morning. We had such a nice time there on Saturday together—it was so relaxing.

Yesterday Uncle Demo gathered two kufas of little pears. So this afternoon we are going to make some of them into sweets.

Now I'll close as Baby must go to bed—she's so fussy most of the time. I'm making fried chicken today. If only you were here with us!

A *kufa* is a round, woven basket about three foot tall. It would hold approximately one and a half bushels.

Chios
Jessie to Costa
August 7, 1963
The people here are terrible about keeping their word. We have been trying to get a plumber here since Saturday morning; the architect also promises and doesn't come, and the man we want for pouring the concrete around the well also doesn't come. None of them keep their promises.

Penny is working on her history—she is about half way through it. I certainly hope she will go into the 5th grade and will do well.

From Kuwait
August 8, 1963
My Darling Jessie,
Sorry about the washing machine. I could make it work down near the well from the mangano current or I could have gotten an extension from there. In any event I am not there so I cannot do it.

I am tentatively leaving here on the 15th of August 10 a.m. to Beirut

18th of August to Geneva and Lausanne, 19th to Barcelona, Barcelona to New York, New York to Chicago 21st of August, Janesville 21st-23rd, Paducah 23rd evening to morning of 26th, Chicago 26 & 27, New York 28th to Sept 4, Sept 5 Geneva to Lausanne, Sept 6th to Athens.

You have not acknowledged receipt of any of my letters from Kuwait yet. I hope the children are alright. I wish I could speak to all of you.

Costa

From Chios
Jessie to Costa
August 15, 1963

Today is YiaYiá's nameday. She understood so this morning but later on in the day she will probably forget. I have bought a nice cake for her which we will have at tea this afternoon. Uncle Mike has gone to church and Penny has gone with him.

Jessie

From Kuwait
Costa to Jessie
August 16, 1963 evening

I could not leave Kuwait on the 15th because the last two days were a mad rush. I am glad that I did not because on the night of the 15th I got from Haji an $86,000 order for Parker which we typed up last night and had him sign this morning....

Najib fouled up the Olds deal. He forgot the keys in Kuwait (he says.) He is a lousy character just as you said. I am trying slowly but surely to cut my relation with him.

I am so sorry my darling that I will not be able to come to Chios now. My time is so short that it is not worth it. Costa

From Kuwait
Costa to Jessie
August 17, 1963

If nothing else, I have gotten in touch with Muntaha and she will come back on the 15th of September or whenever we are back here. So now we have her and Khadija. we shall try to get a driver so that you will not have to do that.

Regarding the boats, I have requested John Tchapourian to book us all on the *Lydia* which leaves Piraeus on the 10th of September. You will have to ship the car on the 6th and book to come to Athens on the 9th to catch the *Lydia*. I have asked John to write to you about the reservations.

Costa

From Chios
Jessie to Costa
August 17, 1963

It's a little late, I know, but while you are in New York, and if you can find it, I would like to have a pretty pink bathing suit. The black

148

one you bought me three years ago has served me so well, and still is, and you had chosen so well when you bought it, that if you could find something nice, I know I would like it. Anyhow, only if you have time, should you trouble to look for anything. I know you have so many things to do there.

Jessie

Costa did bring me a perfect and lovely pink bathing suit.

From Chios
Jessie to Costa
August 19, 1963
We went to Karfas yesterday, but I did not enjoy swimming there very much. What I did enjoy though was Baby. You should have seen her in the water in Stephanie's tube! So this morning, I bought her a little one; Stephanie's is too big for her. She has begun to say quite a lot of new words and you will be surprised when you see and hear her. Also she has learned to climb down from her bed, over chairs and all—this I am not too happy for.

The days are still very hot, but we slept much better last night as we had moved our beds out to the terrace.

Jessie

From Chios
Jessie to Costa
August 22, 1963
I hope the new order of 200 refrigerators and 37 air conditioners

won't come out our noses again. In
any case I guess you had to go ahead
and place the order in order to save
the agency. That would be nice if
Leonard gives the air conditioning
line for Kuwait.

Penny made a grade of 95 on her
history test today. Of course she and
I were both very pleased.

I still don't know which day
exactly you plan to be here, but I
hope you will not be delayed in New
York and can get back quickly so that
you will have a few days to rest here.
Jessie

More refrigerators and air conditioners going to the
bottomless pit in Baghdad.

From Chios
Jessie to Costa
August 25, 1963
I have yesterday received two
letters from you—Beirut of August 17th
and your letter written on the plane
between Geneva and Barcelona.

You say you met Mrs. Albrecht and
Ingrid and they didn't impress you.
Ingrid is very shy which would explain
her quietness, but her mother never
ceases to talk—of course with Mr.
Wagner there, I don't suppose she had
too much of a chance. You really put
it so nicely, "His usual exuberant
self and the center of attraction."

Regarding a TV assembly plant for
Greece—I too think it's a wonderful

idea, especially so if it would mean we could live our lives more together than apart. Undoubtedly you would be in charge of such an operation should it materialize, but what happens to Parker in the Gulf? Who would take care of that?

Katherine has become very naughty the past few days. She gets out of her bed around 5:30 and starts tracking from room to room, back and forth, so I'm afraid that tomorrow morning early, she is going to get her bottom spanked nicely.

Uncle Demo has gone hunting today. He will probably come back with either one sparrow or nothing—and more than likely the latter. Jessie

From Chios
Jessie to Costa
August 26, 1963

It is only in a letter just received day before yesterday that I understood why you went to Barcelona. All the time I was under the impression that you were going there to look into the question of exchange which you spoke to me about in a letter when I was in Schruns. I had no idea that you were going there to see the Zenith plant.

Maybe if you had had a few martinis and me, perhaps you would have been able to remember your Spanish again. In fact, we both might have been able to speak Spanish.

The question of the washing machine
is maddening. We have a new
transformer and it is not a question
of the transformer working, because it
works fine. It is the current and
nothing can be done about it by us.
The machine cannot work continuously—
just stops and starts time and again.
From the beginning I was against the
whole thing. Now I've paid $700 for
something that is half useful. Anyhow
what's done is done. Jessie

Sadly, the TV assembly plant for Greece never
materialized, and we continued to live our lives more apart than
together.

From Chios
Jessie to Costa
August 27, 1963
Yesterday afternoon we collected
all the pine cones. Today they will
be opened, dried a little in the sun.
Then we will crack some of them to
take back to Beirut. The almonds we
finished cracking and cleaning Sunday.
There weren't really an awful lot.
Uncles tell me there were many more
last year. It was the same in '59
when we were here. The crop was "all
so very much better last year." The
only crops that are better this year
are the flies, mosquitoes and fleas.
Uncle Demo took the children on the
donkey yesterday late in the afternoon
to his mountain and they enjoyed that
a lot. Jessie

Early September, Costa came back to Chios. In a few days we were all packed up with the car, ready to take the ship to Athens (Piraeus). There we boarded another ship for Beirut. I believe it was the *Lydia*.

Constantine John, II

You may strive to be like them, but seek not to make them like you.
For life goes not backward nor tarries with yesterday.

Kahlil Gibran

By the second week of September we were back in Beirut, and Penny and Stephanie began the school year at the American Community School. My health was still poor. I was constantly tired, impatient, short-tempered, and could not seem to recover. However, Costa wanted us to have another son.

I said, " Costa I'm not well."

"Well then we'll adopt," he said.

In October 1963, he asked our good friend, Alex the obstetrician to look out for a baby boy that we could adopt. About a month later, early November, Alex phoned. He asked, "Where's Costa?"

"He's in Kuwait."

"When is he coming back?"

"I don't know, maybe next week."

"Well call him, and tell him to come now. I found a baby boy here at the Khaldi Hospital."

"Did you deliver him?"

"No , but he is available if you want him."

"Okay, I'll call him." So I phoned Costa immediately and told him the news.

"Well, go and get him," Costa said.

"Costa, he's not a sack of sugar or a bag of flour," I said. "Come home. Tomorrow." And he did so, the following day.

With Alex, we went to see the baby. After dressing him, we went directly to the Crèche, the orphanage in Beirut, where we spent about a half an hour doing paperwork with the Sisters there. A priest was involved, who was helping us, but I no longer remember his name. He did not accompany us to the Crèche but had given us instructions to follow for the adoption.

Our new son was a tiny baby, born premature, and not too healthy. He had been, since birth, neglected at the hospital. As far as we knew, he was 11 days old. The staff at Khaldi Hospital could not give us his actual birth date. One of the nurses said to me, "Why are you doing all this extra work? Just take him home." We certainly did not feel this was the correct. We wanted to do this properly and legitimately.

After finishing the formalities, we took him home, gave him the birth date of November 5th, and soon christened him Constantine John Halkias II. We called him John.

> Beirut
> December 10, 1963
> My Darling Costa,
> This whole day I have wanted so very much to phone you but you told me before that it was better if you phoned me from there. Also, I'm not sure that you are in Kuwait.
> The children are just fine and John is becoming more lovely each day. I have waited such a long time—eleven years—for him to come back to me. You will see how beautiful he is.
> Today I didn't go out except to chose our Christmas tree. I stayed home and rested most of the day, and I feel a bit better tonight. Since last Thursday I've been rather dragged out.
> Tomorrow, I'll try to go to the office and maybe try to get some filing in order. Depends on how I feel.
> Seems like you have been gone for months and months. I hope the next ten

days will pass quickly and you will be back
home with us.
        Jessie

In December I lost a dear friend. I had known her in Baghdad all the eight years living there. Peggy was sexually molested and stabbed 27 times with a butcher knife. Whoever was responsible for this heinous crime had been sitting with her in her living room drinking coffee. Surely it was someone she had known well and trusted.

Peggy had a great influence on my life in Baghdad when I was young and newly married. She taught me so many things—how to *survive*, how to cook (even without Crisco and wax paper!)—all kinds of things. She even taught me to make my own yogurt since it could not be bought from the grocery shop. She had been my mother's age and had been such a crutch for me when I was young. Her husband, Vincent, and Costa were like brothers—very best friends, and we lived only five minutes apart.

Her daughter Vivi arrived home from work to find her mother dead. Not surprisingly, the murder was never solved. Often, I pass the building where Peggy lived and died. It was easy to get away with murder in Beirut, but despite that, I never was concerned for our safety while living there.

By 1964, Costa began to broaden his range of travel throughout the Arab countries which encompassed Abu Dhabi, Qatar, Bahrain, Dubai, and at times Saudi Arabia. Much of his business was importing merchandise and selling to the *entrepôt*[6] market in Iran, India, and Saudi

---

[6]An entrepôt is a trading post where merchandise can be imported and exported without paying import duties, often at a profit. To illustrate, the reluctance of ships to travel the entire length of a long trading route made them more willing to sell to an

Arabia, and at times even little Oman. A great deal of contraband left Kuwait. Regularly, ships and dhows (sailing vessels) plied the waters between Kuwait and Iran as well as India.

Besides his office in Kuwait, Costa eventually opened one up in Dubai. In the early '70s he was beginning a close business relationship with a Saudi firm. For the next 30 years, he would be deeply involved in business throughout most of the Arab countries, traveling extensively, not only in the Middle East, but Europe, the Far East, and the United States.

During the next two years, I finished, through correspondence, three courses in interior design. The first and second were with the University of Minnesota; the third was with the New York School of Interior Design. It was during the 1950s when I realized that my dream (well, one of them!) was to study Interior Design. But how? The years passed. In the early 1960s I learned that the University of Minnesota offered the study of Interior Design by correspondence. Maybe it could happen after all. We now had four children, I had recovered from hepatitis, and we were living in Beirut, Lebanon.

By letter, I inquired about the program offered by the University of Minnesota. Promptly and positively the University answered me. I was delighted and enrolled immediately into their program by correspondence. With all the necessary formalities completed, my home study program began.

---

entrepôt instead. The entrepôt then sells the goods at a higher price to ships travelling the other segment of the route. In modern times customs areas have largely made such entrepôts obsolete. This type of port should not be confused with the modern French usage of the word entrepôt meaning warehouse.

http://en.wikipedia.org/wiki/Entrepôts

Lesson by lesson was completed, mailed in, graded, and returned to me. I believe there were 25 in total. Every two weeks, a lesson would be completed (my schedule) and returned. Probably, I spent 25 to 30 hours on each lesson. My lowest grade received was an A-. I was overjoyed with my efforts, and loved each and every minute of my study. In well less than a year, I had completed Design I.

My instructor, Leah Lewis, and I became good friends. Greatly encouraged, I registered for Design II. By early 1965, I was on my way to studying Design II. Leah Lewis again was my instructor. Again, I was a model student. One time I earned only a B+ on a lesson and quivered! However, within two years I had earned an Associate Degree in Interior Design.

A few months later, I learned that the New York School of Interior Design (NYSID) offered correspondence as well. I made contact with NYSID and signed up. As I recall this course lasted about a year and comprised of 20 to 30 lessons. Again my grades were all As. I could only be pleased.

In 1966, while in New York, and having recently completed my correspondence program and earning a certificate from NYSID, I paid a visit to the school.

Upon arrival, the receptionist asked, "How can I help you?"

My answer was, "I have recently completed a correspondence program with your school, and I am passing by to say 'hello.'"

"Just a minute," she answered and walked away.

She returned with a person who said to me, "If you are looking for work, we cannot help you," then turned and walked away.

I was insulted, shocked, and disgusted. Nothing I had said or done had invited this behavior. I have always wanted to put this in writing; now I have done so.

While taking these correspondence courses, my friend Giselle al-Askari was also studying interior design by correspondence with a school in Paris. We had been friends since years before in Iraq. So as long as we both were in love with the subject, it was only natural for us to study and compare notes together.

The studying in Beirut proved most useful throughout the years, as Costa and I engaged in the remodeling of the house in Chios, the villa in Kuwait, and the properties we bought and sold in Florida, New Hampshire, Cairo, Maine, Cyprus, Boston and Washington.

In the month of May, 1965, we were invited to our good friend Ed McCray's (Parker Pen Company) wedding in Hong Kong. We promptly accepted. Off we went, my first visit to the Far East, where we spent a fascinating and beautiful ten days.

Ed was marrying a Chinese girl from Swatow. Before we had left for the wedding, our Beirut friend, Mr. Halim Hanna, had said to me, "In America there are 200 million people, and 100 million of them are women. Why does Ed need to go all the way to Hong Kong for a wife?" I am still close to the Hanna family.

Stopping in Bangkok on the return, most of all I recall the wonderful and plentiful selection of silks, designed by the world-famous Jim Thompson, an American business man living in Thailand, who had been responsible for reviving the silk industry a number of years before.

In 1967, two years after our visit to Bangkok, while on holiday in Malaysia, Jim Thompson was out for a stroll near the jungle. He never returned. There is speculation that his body was hidden in an unmarked grave after a hit and run accident, but to this date it is a mystery what happened to this man.

Athens (1967-1968)

In 1967, the Arab-Israeli conflict broke out into what became known as the Six-Day War or June War. Although Lebanon played no active role in the conflict, Palestinians were using Lebanon as a base for attacks against Israel. Since Costa felt we were no longer safe in Beirut, we decided that the children and I would leave the country, go first to Athens, and then on to Chios.

We were to travel by ship to Limassol (Cyprus), thence to the Port of Athens (Piraeus) via Alexandria. It would become a memorable trip, to say the least. The children and I would be traveling on a Greek ship, along with 14 pieces of luggage, a car, a sailboat, and two bicycles. Our clearing agent Yves Berberian and Costa were at the Beirut Port to see us off. That evening we had our dinner on the ship, and it was late by the time we sat down. I had already given the children dinner and settled them in for the night. Berberian and Costa left the ship immediately after dinner. It was 10 p.m. when we sailed.

At 5:00 a.m. the following morning, there was a loud knock on the door of my cabin. "Get up. You must leave the ship."

All I could think was: *We are sinking!*

Instead, I was told, "We are not going to Alexandria. We are going to Limassol, and you must leave this ship. Get your children and your overnight bags ready. Everything else you will leave on the ship."

Apparently, our ship had been sequestered by the military to go to Alexandria because of the war situation. Well, okay. Leave the car, bicycles, pieces of luggage, sailboat, everything? I roused the children and made ready to leave, and by seven o'clock we were off the ship.

We were near Limassol, but the sea was too shallow for the ship to dock, so lighters were brought out to take us to shore. A lighter is a flat-bottomed barge used to transfer goods and passengers to and from moored ships. I loaded up the children with a piece or two of luggage, wondering if I would ever again see the car, sailboat or any of our other belongings! We were taken to a café on the dusty beachfront, a confined area with ancient wooden chairs and tables under the pine trees—the most uncomfortable surroundings imaginable. We stayed there the full day. How do you *hang out* for more than twelve hours in such a small area with four young ones? Penny was fourteen years old; Stephanie nearly ten, Katherine almost six, and John would be four in November.

Altogether we were probably 175 persons waiting on the beach. We were given coffee, lunch, water and other cold drinks, but, with absolutely nothing to do the entire day, we sat and waited like refugees.

Finally at about eight o'clock that night, we were herded back onto the lighters and onto a different ship called the *Achilles* another Greek ship. I do not remember the name of the ship we had taken from Beirut, but the *Achilles* was much nicer than the one we were obliged to abandon. We were directed to enter the ship from the cargo entrance. A man was sitting at a table, processing the passengers. The line was long and slow. By then both John and Katherine were on the floor crying—as well as dirty, hungry, and very tired.

I broke line. This was not my style, but I had become desperate. I told Penny, "You stay here with them." Stepping up to the processor at the table, I said, "Look, I have four young children. The two youngest are exhausted. You must get us as quickly as possible into some cabins."

He understood my desperation. He asked my name and immediately assigned us three cabins. We located our cabins; I washed Katherine's and John's faces and hands, put them to bed, and told Stephanie to stand guard until Penny and I returned. Off we went to retrieve *kit, cat, sacks, and lives*, tho we surely were not going to St. Ives.

First we found the car. It was fine. Then up to the deck. We found a huge, I mean *huge* heap of mixed up luggage and belongings, simply dumped all together. Miraculously, we located every single piece, including the bicycles and sailboat. By then it was after ten. Back to the little ones' cabin we went, to find Stephanie asleep. Penny and I went to the dining room where we enjoyed a nice dinner. What a day it had been!

For two days and nights we were on the *Achilles*. It was not the *Queen Mary*; however, it was a much nicer ship than the one out of Beirut. *And* there was a nice swimming pool.

When we docked at Piraeus, Costa's sister Maria and her husband Vassily were waiting for us, and took us to their house for lunch. Upon arrival back at Piraeus late afternoon, all our belongings—car and all—had been safely transferred from the *Achilles* to the Chios-bound ship, and perfectly stowed in their proper places. This was all thanks to Vassily, the ex-merchant marine.

We traveled to Chios and stayed on for six or eight weeks. Costa and I exchanged letters until he could join us.

```
Chios
August 6, 1967
My Darling Costa,
     It is seven in the evening and I'm all
alone in the house.  Uncle Mike has gone
to town and Uncle Demo, Kiki and the
children have gone to church.  I sit here
writing to you, missing you something
awfully, and boiling the milk...
     The mother cat has abandoned her
kitten.  The dog has adopted it; she puts
it into her house, nurses it and looks
after it as though it were her own.  It is
quite a sight! And cute as can be.
     Better I put an end to this
uninteresting piece of missive, and tell
you that I love you so very much; am
counting the days (as though I knew how
many) until you come back.
     Jessie
```

Costa arrived. We remained another ten days, and then all together returned to Athens by ship. Air service had started by this time, but with the car and so many belongings, it would have been impossible to travel by plane.

The moment we arrived in Athens, I despised being there. It wasn't just Greece. Costa had gone earlier and rented a house for us. I did not at all like the house! Besides disliking the house, I disliked the location, the landlord, and the distances from anything pleasant. The year in Athens was a most unhappy time for me.

Penny, Stephanie, and Katherine were enrolled in the American Community school of Athens, and John began kindergarten there. Costa's sisters and mother kept their distance and only came around to check on me occasionally. This was mostly, I believe, to find out exactly what I was doing. There was no friendship between Maria's two children and Penny and Stephanie, even though they were close in age.

The house we lived in was halfway underground and built for two families. The downstairs was built like a mother-in-law apartment and was where the Lebanese maids had their quarters. They, too, were unhappy. I could not keep the younger maid off the street. She was constantly at the front gate to see what or who was passing by. Although she could not understand a word being said, she continued going out. A problem.

I wasn't doing any housework or cooking, nothing of the sort. I guess I was just bored. I had no friends there except one couple, but they were both working full time, and I rarely saw them. There was no one.

Our office was downstairs also, and I had to go outside to get there which wasn't pleasant. The landlord was a nasty fellow. There was a fig tree in the back yard, and we weren't allowed to touch those figs, not even if they fell on the ground. The weather was unpleasant; I became ill.

Occasionally one of our Beirut friends would pass through Athens, and I would receive a phone call. Al Buckley, the manager of Chase Manhattan Bank in Beirut at that time, called one day. I was so happy to hear from him—someone from Beirut! Al was staying at the Hilton. In those days everybody stayed at the Hilton. He took a taxi out to see me. When he got there, he asked me what he could do for me in Beirut and I said, "Just find me an apartment in Beirut. I'm going to come back with the children." That was in late fall.

Costa would come and stay a few days or a week and leave again. He spent most of his time in the Gulf. It was a two-hour flight from Kuwait to Beirut, and when we lived in Beirut, he would come home for two or three days at a time, but it was a four-hour flight from Kuwait to Athens and was too far to come home for short visits. We didn't see him too often.

```
Kuwait
January 16, 1968
My Darling Jessie,
    I love you very much and on this day
more than any other I feel very lonely and
wish I could be near you.  I have been
remembering the day of our second wedding
and how lovely everything was.  I hope that
14 years have not changed your hopes of
that lovely day at Baghdad College.  As
human beings we might do things that are
wrong as far as other human beings are
concerned.  Whatever you say we have had
so far a very good life together.  My hope
and my aspirations will be that we would
make our life a little more pleasant, a
little more interesting, a little more
exciting for 1968.  I love you Jessie very
much and hope that 14 years from now, we
are still on earth and together enjoying a
lovely family of boys and girls that will
be coming after us, which we will enjoy
guiding and advising. Costa
```

This was our 16th anniversary in January (not the 14th as he says in the letter), but he was doing his best from afar to keep me in is thoughts. I was still trying to stay in contact with Costa's sisters and mother, but it wasn't going well, and I seldom saw our friends George and Vera.

> January 31, 1968
> Athens
> My Darling Costa,
> Yesterday I had my Greek lesson. After the lesson I went to see your mother and Thalia. They were not there when I arrived, but Margie was, so I went in and waited. They returned about twenty minutes later, and I only stayed ten or fifteen minutes. Thalia was fine, but your mother seemed unhappy which has been the case the past two or three times I have gone there. Also she seemed surprised to hear that you were not here.
> I have seen and talked to George and Vera very little during the past two or three weeks. Their maid was away for two weeks so they were very busy at home. Vera was quite upset that she was having so much to do so I tried to keep quiet and not disturb them any more than absolutely necessary. That is our news. Jessie

Telephone conversations were almost impossible, and the distance between us was becoming more and more difficult for me.

> February 3, 1968
> Beirut
> My Darling Jessie,
> Yesterday I finally managed to talk to you but again you were not happy with me.

167

I do not blame you as I have been gone over a month.

In Beirut I have been running like mad. Unfortunately I could not get back to Kuwait last night on the Kuwait Airways planes are fully booked until next Wednesday.

I love all of you very much and think of you constantly. By the way I've been on the wagon since the 23rd of January. Hope I'll stay that way for many years.

Please don't be mad at me. Love you very much. Costa

February 3rd 1968
En route to Abadan
My Darling Jessie,
Needless to say I have noticed that you are not happy in Greece, for many reasons. To name a few:

1. I'm away longer than when we were in Beirut.

2. You are not working on things like you used to in Beirut.

3. You do not have the group of friends that you had in Beirut.

4. My family has not changed after all these years.

Jessie I love you very much and want you and the children to be happy, safe and comfortable. You have to be completely frank with me on this point so that I can also be safe in taking a decision that it will be the correct one all around.

One of the topics I will discuss at Sheaffer would be to be put on a salary basis until John gets his papers in order and becomes a little American like the rest of us. For the life of me, however I do not know what good it will do him. I believe in destiny and would prefer to leave him a Lebanese. Again we have to discuss this point when I come back on Saturday the 19ᵗʰ of February.

When I got back to Beirut two days ago, our house telephone was not working. The same excuse was made that the inside lines were chewed up by a rat. I raised a big fuss and within half an hour the line was returned and I believe there is someone that uses our line during my long absences.

As I told you on the telephone Antoine Assi was murdered in cold blood and his store robbed of ££500,000[7] worth of jewelry. The police have caught the murderers. They are these Armenian thugs.

The whole business community of Beirut was closed yesterday in protest against the government's lax laws in treating with criminals. It saddened me because I had done business with him a few weeks ago when he fixed the diamonds for you and my pens. Really it is so easy to get away with murder in Beirut. Costa

That winter in Greece, I was ill and didn't know why. No appetite—nothing; I just wanted to stay in bed.

February 24, 1968
Athens
Jessie to Costa
It is now three weeks that I am in this useless condition. I do believe that if I

---

[7] 1967-68 exchange rate ££3=$1 U.S

do not soon regain my strength, that I
shall certainly go mad. When I am all
right, there are times that I think I shall
lose my mind, but these last few weeks it
has been ten times worse. Jessie

Finally Costa arrived in Athens. He phoned our friend and doctor, Na'aman Boustany, in Beirut. Na'aman told him to give me *this and that*, but nothing made a difference. I did not know what we were going to do, so I returned to my bed. It was March of 1968. I told Costa, "I am going to die here. I cannot bear this."

We shortly left for Beirut for a visit to see our doctor. He examined me, but could find nothing wrong. Simply, I was homesick and lonely. With no friends to speak of, the children and the maids were all I had. Costa would drop in occasionally, but he was obliged to spend most of his time in the Gulf.

As he had business there, we did travel to Frankfurt that winter and Costa bought me a mink coat. It was of little use, however. I was feeling ill and had no place to wear it.

One good thing that came out of that year for me was that I quit smoking. Also, I studied the piano diligently and spent much time practicing, which served as a distraction during that miserable year in Greece. Unfortunately, I haven't played much since.

When June, 1968 arrived, we packed up all four children and boarded the *Stella Oceanis* for a ten-day cruise through the Greek islands and to Istanbul. It was all very nice. Wherever we landed, Penny and Stephanie came along with us sightseeing because they could manage well with the walking. Katherine and John, however, were only seven and five; we were obliged to leave them on the ship. Though they were well-cared for, both created more than a scene: "Can we go? Are we going? Why can't we go?" Perhaps we did not need to bring the younger ones along, but I simply didn't want to leave them home. In all respects the ship was lovely, accommodations excellent, and the food was fantastic. It was beautiful to visit more of the Islands as well as to see a bit of Istanbul.

Still, I did not want to live in Greece.

Beirut (1968-1975)

In July, 1968, we moved back to Beirut. We needed to find an apartment since we had given up the one we had when we left a year earlier. The people who took our old apartment (they still live there) were good friends. We did find a lovely apartment, very spacious with a sea view, and with many friends in the area.

We kept this apartment until 1994, even though we were more permanently situated in Kuwait during the Lebanese civil war which lasted from 1975 to 1990.

Costa and I were still having a difficult time. Being a jealous man, and the fact that he was away so much, just added fuel to the fire.

July 7, 1968
Beirut
My Darling Jessie,

I came home for a few hours to be with all of you which is the first and foremost of my dreams and unfortunately we had to have words again. Words about nothing. I am sorry that I was angry with you but then it was a spoilt weekend. I am sorry.

With love to all of you. Costa

I love no one but you. Please do not bring up this again. All our troubles start from the fact that I love you too much. Costa

July 12, 1968
Athens
Dearest Costa,

Just as you said, "home for a few hours...unfortunately we had to have words again. Words about nothing...then it was a spoilt weekend."

When and where will this sort of thing ever end? Why is it for one reason or another (and maybe not a reason) I am being driven to the point so often of screeching like a fishmonger's wife? Can't we ever sit down and discuss *anything* and reach a sensible solution or conclusion? Why are things so often left hanging in mid-air, undecided? What's the matter?

I am saying these things to you on paper because this way you may listen to me. In person it would undoubtedly be otherwise. There is no point in getting annoyed with me—it will neither do good nor bad. Plainly, I feel that you can no longer be bothered with my simpleminded thoughts and or words. If you feel like answering me, I would appreciate it in the form of answers, not questions.

Congratulations to Aly for his second daughter. He may even have a third one, and there is nothing bad about that. Girls are certainly just as fine as boys.

As always I enjoy every word of your letters, reading them again and again. You may think I have spoken too openly and straightforward. If I'm going to say what I feel, I know no other way. I love you with all my heart. I do not want to hurt you—neither do I want to be hurt.
    Your Jessie

It was in 1968 when Costa joined the Quraishi brothers in Saudi Arabia. The Quaraishis wanted the Carreras Cigarette Agency in the worst way as the cigarette business was really big in the country at that time. Costa had recently met and become friends with John Cook, an ex-British Army officer, who was now the Carreras representative for the Middle East. John was based in Bahrain, where he lived with his wife, Lexi. Perhaps that is where they met; in any case, they became acquainted somewhere in the Gulf. The obtainment of this agency for Saudi Arabia was through the sole efforts and connections of Costa. (When Costa became ill in 1999, I was disappointed with the settlement we received for his work over all the years he spent with the Quraishi Brothers, but I accepted it and moved on.)

In mid-July of 1969, Costa and I flew to London, where he attended meetings with the Carreras people. Within a few days we returned to Rome. At Civitavecchia, the port of Rome, we rented a small car to take with us on the ship to Olbia, the port of the Island of Sardinia where we had planned to spend ten days. It was the Costa

Esmeralda Coast at Porto Cervo where the likes of the Aga Khan, Princess Margaret, and Bridgette Bardot passed their summers. Upon landing, we headed to the Porto Cervo Hotel (Costa Esmeralda Resort), with the Mediterranean style décor and private beach. To this day, the Cervo Hotel remains the number one hotel/resort on Sardinia.

During our stay at Porto Cervo, the first U.S. moon landing took place. In those days, none of the rooms in the Cervo were provided with television sets. There was a television in the bar—no more no less. We were informed by the manager that in order to view the expected moon landing that evening, we would need to meet together in the bar. Thus we all gathered there at the given time. Some of us on chairs, many on the floor, awaiting this spectacular and historical event. At 4:18 p.m. EDT, July 20, 1969 (10:18 p.m. in Sardinia) the Eagle landed on the moon. Six hours later Neil Armstrong stepped onto the surface of the moon.

We did not remain our allotted time at the Cervo (pronounced chevro) on Sardinia. Laundry was the issue. A week's time was needed to be given for the laundry/dry cleaning to go and come, and we needed fresh clothes sooner than later, having spent time in London and Rome. We decided to return to Rome where we checked in at the Parco dei Principi Grand Hotel within the Villa Borghese Park. There we remained four days before returning to Beirut. Besides getting our laundry in order, we visited my old American Embassy friend, Pat Comber, from the Baghdad days. She lived with her family in the Vatican Park Apartments in close proximity to the Cavalieri Hilton.

```
September 1, 1969
Beirut
My Darling Costa,
    By having you with me for nearly two
months I became very spoiled having you
```

near me and looking after me. As a result
of this I am now ever lonely and must
stretch my shoulders out in order to carry
some of the responsibility again.

In the early spring of 1970, while at the office, for some reason I
looked up to the ceiling. Obviously, something was wrong with my left
eye. The doctor put me on cortisone. I spent five days at the American
University of Beirut hospital (AUB) and soon broke out in herpes on the
left side of my head. Cortisone was immediately discontinued. End
result: 20% vision in my left eye was lost.

> April 4, 1970
> Kuwait
> My Darling Jessie,
> May good luck be with you today. May
> your tests show that there is nothing
> serious and that your eye will get better
> quickly. Please do not worry, we are all
> your eyes and we love you very much so
> cheer up.

Costa and I had long spoken of driving north from Beirut through
Turkey, and up the western coast to Izmir, thence to Çeşme where we
could ferry over to Chios. Our plan was to spend three weeks as a family
on our island. It was August 1970.

By the end of the first day, we had reached Antalya on Turkey's
southern coast. It was late in the afternoon, and we were all of course
very tired. Stopping at a so-called motel directly on the beach, we
found it adequate—no more, no less. However, the air was thick with
mosquitoes—so thick, one could not know if it was day or night.
(Antalya is much changed since that day in August. It has become a

well-known five-star resort—far different than the Antalya we visited in 1970.)

The following day we continued on to Izmir and found our way to the Buyuk Efes Hotel. We needed three rooms, but no rooms were available, only suites. We rented three suites—all on different floors! John and Katherine were in a suite, Penny and Stephanie in another, and Costa and I stayed in the third. It was very late at night but comfortable for sleeping. The following morning we resumed our trip in the direction of Çeşme where we found the ferry waiting to take us to Chios.

We did remain for three weeks. During that time, Costa and I took a week's trip, by ferry with our car, to Mytilene or Lesbos.[8] The children remained in Chios.

On the return trip to Beirut, we crossed the interior of Turkey, going through Konya, before heading southward and back home to Beirut. Before leaving Beirut, Costa was thoroughly convinced that traveling through Turkey was dangerous, and we may surely all be murdered. No such thing—not even a chance. I have always been happy we made this trip—it was a special time.

In the fall of 1970, Bill Polk and his friend, Larry Perkins (the Chicago architectural firm of Perkins and Will) appeared in Beirut. They were en route to Teheran, then on to Kabul. After a few days in

---

[8]The word lesbian is derived from the name of the Greek island of Lesbos, home to the 6th-century BCE poet Sappho. From various ancient writings, historians gathered that a group of young women were left in Sappho's charge for their instruction or cultural edification. Little of Sappho's poetry remains, but her remaining poetry reflects the topics she wrote about: women's daily lives, their relationships, and rituals. She focused on the beauty of women and proclaimed her love for girls. Before the late 19th century, the word lesbian referred to any derivative or aspect of Lesbos, including a type of wine.
http://en.wikipedia.org/wiki/Lesbian

Beirut, Bill said to us, "Why don't you go with us to Teheran and Kabul?" We did.

After three days at the Teheran Hilton, with beautiful people, great parties, and with a bit of sightseeing mixed in, the four of us flew to Kabul.

Upon arrival in Kabul, Bill told us that we would be having dinner that evening with his friend, Dr. Dupree, an archaeologist, and his wife, at their home. That would be fine. Upon arrival at the front door, Mrs. Dupree greeted us. The moment we looked at each other, we announced simultaneously, "I know you." Nancy had been the wife of a different man during our Baghdad days. Small world! After that evening, we never met again.

The following day, with Bill and Larry, in a caravan of four cars, as guests of the Deputy Prime Minister, we were taken on a sightseeing trip with a picnic lunch into the Hindu Kush. These mountains are located near the borders of Afghanistan with Pakistan, Tajikistan, as well as China and form part of the Himalayan foothills. The rugged scenery was overwhelming.

The following day, we were entertained with *Buzkashi. Buzkashi* (Persian for goat dragging) is the Central Asian sport in which horse mounted players attempt to drag the headless goat or calf carcass toward a goal. It is the national sport of Afghanistan, although it was banned under the Taliban regime. Traditionally, games could last for several days, but in its more regulated tournament version, it has a limited match time.

Costa and I did have time on our own when Bill and Larry were engaged in meetings. A car and driver were at our disposal and showed us around the city a bit—not particularly exciting, as I recall. Overall, however, it was a great trip, and we were most fortunate for the opportunity.

Bill had been busy since he and Costa first met on the *Marine Carp* in 1946 and became fast friends. He has written many books and articles on the Middle East, including *Understanding Iraq: The Whole Sweep of Iraqi History, from Genghis Khan's Mongols to the Ottoman Turks to the British Mandate to the American Occupation.* He currently is married to Baroness Elisabeth von Oppenheimer. Bill and Elizabeth live in the South of France where he continues to spend his time writing articles and books on the Middle East.

In April of 1971, some Beirut friends of ours told me they were going to join, within a week, a tour group coming out of Damascus en route to Moscow. There would be a few passengers collected in Beirut. Immediately I got details, as well as permission from Costa, and went to work on my Russian visa, a ticket on Aeroflot, and a reservation with the tour director. The trip lasted two weeks.

On April 29th we flew to Moscow. The overall trip took in Moscow, St. Petersburg (then called Leningrad) and Riga in Latvia. The weather was cold, and snow was still on the ground. The poorly heated hotel was not the best. May 1st, International Workers' Day, was a very important holiday. All guests of the hotel were obliged to go to the street to be on hand for the *big* parade. The wind was raw; I had developed a cold, and my coat was not warm enough. Memories of this particular outing are not pleasant.

The museums, however, were marvelous, and the Bolshoi entertained us more than once. The State Armory in Moscow was not only interesting, but beautiful, and the visit to Lenin's Tomb was a must do. There was plenty of ballet of course, and we enjoyed *Swan Lake* no less than three times, *The Nutcracker* at least once, as well as various other stage performances. There is an old expression, "It was more fun than a Russian Circus." One of the evenings we spent admiring these fabulous performers. We became true believers!

St. Petersburg architecturally is a beautiful city located on the Neva River. Of course we visited the State Hermitage, one of the oldest and largest museums of art and culture in the world. It was founded in 1767, by Catherine the Great and has been open to the public since 1852. At the time of my visit, unfortunately, the building was sorely in need of extensive refurbishing. Now, however, this has all changed for the better.

We also spent time in Riga, the capitol of Latvia. It is a small city situated on the Baltic Sea. We were handsomely entertained while in Russia, but I lost weight. Except for the ice cream, which was delicious, the food was abominable. As grateful as I was for the trip and as much as I enjoyed it, I was happy to get back to the children and the warm sunshine of Beirut.

In June of 1971, Penny graduated from the American Community School of Beirut. She had applied and was accepted at St. Louis University into their physical therapy program. She and I left for Rome to spend a week at the beautiful Cavalieri Hilton before traveling to the States. This hotel is situated on 15 acres of private Mediterranean parkland with a huge flower and shrubbery garden, overlooking the Eternal City. I wanted to take Penny to Rome because I knew she would benefit from it; she enjoys culture, paintings, art and all that sort of thing. While in Rome, I got a chance to again visit with my old Baghdad friend Pat which was another plus of course.

Penny and I paid our respects to St. Peter's, the Vatican, and enjoyed a performance of *Aida* with live elephants in the Villa Borghese Park. This was needless to say grand. We also took a full day and traveled by train to Florence to visit the Uffizi Palace Museum, one of the oldest and most famous museums of the Western World.

Besides sightseeing and entertaining Penny in Rome (we both loved being there), I was looking for a diamond. We made a number of trips to the jeweler Bulgari where a few years earlier Costa had bought for me a blue sapphire surrounded by diamonds which I dearly loved. Since this year was our 20th wedding anniversary, I had been told to go to Bulgari to find the right ring. Of the two brothers, it was Nicholas with whom I was dealing with this time.

```
June 18, 1971
     Jessie, When will you learn that it is
not a shame to bargain. I've just talked
to you and I am disappointed in you. After
all these years haven't you learned how to
do it? How many people walk into Bulgari's
and buy $16,000 rings? He'll bend.   Not
you.   With   love   from   your   bargaining
husband.   Costa
```

While Penny and I were traveling, Costa cared for the rest of the children, in both Beirut and Jeddah.

```
July 28, 1971
Beirut
Costa to Jessie
Dearest Darling,
     Everything   has   been   going   very
smoothly.   The children are all fine and
miss you very much.   So do I.
```

181

I've played the role of cook with the very able assistant of Katherine who has already fixed one breakfast and made an apple pie. Since she had a good teacher I'm sure it will be excellent. We had spaghetti yesterday. We are having rice and chili today and so it goes. Something different every day.

Tomorrow we will know about the Visa for Jeddah and will definitely write to you about our trip. I'll cable you when we leave.

I hope you have succeeded in buying your diamond...

After numerous bargaining sessions with Nicholas and two phone calls to Costa, I ended up with exactly what I wanted.

July 28, 1971
Dear Mommy and Penny,
How is your trip? How is Rome? Are you having a good time? We are. And I wish that you were here to eat my pie. Give my love to Grandma and Grampa when you get there. Love, Katherine.

After a week in Rome, and sated with so many of the greatest memorials of all time, the world's loveliest hotels, delicious food and wine, we left for the States. After spending a few weeks with my mother in Kentucky, we made our way to St. Louis for Penny to enter St. Louis University.

While Penny and I were in Rome and the States, Costa took the children to Jeddah, on the Red Sea, in Saudi Arabia.

August 7, 1971
My Dearest Jessie,
The children and I arrived in Jeddah on
the 2nd of August and settled into our small
smelly apartment. We have been here five
days and have survived. Humidity is the
only discomfort particularly when you get
into a car standing in the sun...
The children and I have had a lot of
fun. We have been to the Creek twice, to
play tennis at the Dunes Club once, to
visit with the Thomases once. Today we
had lunch at Khaled. This evening Kathy
Moore is arriving and I guess one more or
less will not make much difference...

The Creek is an arm extending inland from the Red Sea towards
Jeddah. It is very shallow but drops off unexpectedly when wading out
into it. Stephanie's friend Kathy Moore joined them in Jeddah, so Costa
had two 13-year-olds, as well as Katherine who was ten and John, eight.

August 13, 1971
Jeddah
We spent the day at the Creek. Enclosed
are some pictures of some Arabs who are
your children. I finally received your
letter from Rome together with postcard
from you and Penny. Have not attempted to
call yet. I'll do so soon. With love to
all of you. Costa

They went swimming every day. Katherine made her father
another pie and blew up the oven while Penny and I were in Rome
enjoying ourselves.

August 20, 1971
Jeddah
My Darling Jessie,

I'm glad you like your diamond. To me it represents the best for the best there is. It shows that after twenty years we love each other more—it shows that we are special. What else can I say. Needless to say I wish I were with you on your trip to Iowa and Moline.

Poor Katherine had an accident with our gas stove two days after we arrived in Jeddah. She was trying to do something and did not know how to light the stove and it blew up in her face and singed her hair and burned her already sun burnt nose. She was more scared than anything else. They are both menaces. John is a holy terror. One has to watch him 24 hours so that he does not kill himself. He is enjoying the shop in Jeddah and everyone of course treats him like the boss's son. Like I was.

I let Stephanie and Kathie Moore loose on some Wolsey samples and they went wild. you will see when you get back to Beirut. We all have chosen things for you. We are even going to send Penny something.
Costa

Penny was now in the States, and Stephanie decided she didn't wish to continue at the American Community School in Beirut. We took her to Switzerland in the summer of 1972 and enrolled her in the Château Beau-Cedre, a boarding school for girls in Montreux, a town perhaps 50 to 60 miles east of Geneva. The school was a very fine, sheltered school located on the shores of Lake Geneva. There, Stephanie finished her last two years of high school.

We had six duty-free shops at the Beirut Airport and in 1973 traveled to Milan in order to buy items for our gold shop. While in Milan, we attended the opera *Die Walküre* at the La Scala. Costa purchased two tickets in the sixth row and had paid the earth for those tickets. My dressmaker had made for me, out of Chinese silk, a simple white sheath with long sleeves and slits up the sides. A hat maker in Beirut made a turban out of the left over fabric. (I loved her work, and had a number of turbans made by this hat-maker.) We were exhausted when we left Beirut, and *Die Walküre* was a heavy opera. I sat there in my white gown and turban, and fell fast asleep for nearly the entire performance.

The real highlight of our stay in Milan was the visit to see one of the world's most famous paintings, *The Last Supper* by Leonardo de Vinci, which is located in the refectory of the convent of Santa Maria delle Grazie, painted between 1494-1498. A fine account of this great piece of art can be found on Wikipedia.

After three days, we took the train from the station, a gorgeous building completed by Mussolini in 1931, into Switzerland. Arriving at a small village, we went by taxi up to Crans where Stephanie and her classmates were staying at the school's ski cottage during the February break. After our short visit with Stephanie at Crans, we were in the taxi back to the train station, and on to Geneva for a few days. Our trips were always a mixture of business with pleasure.

It was 1973, and war was beginning (one more time!) in the Middle East. Syria and Egypt attacked Israel on Yom Kippur, the holiest day of the Jewish calendar, catching Israel off guard. Other Arab countries sent troops to reinforce the Egyptians and Syrians. In addition, the OPEC countries enforced an oil embargo on the industrial nations, including the U.S., Japan and Western Europe. The price of oil increased fourfold and was used as a political weapon to gain support against Israel. Tensions were high between the U.S. and Russia.

The tension from these conflicts spilled over into Beirut. Automobiles and other vehicles, were being stolen, left and right. Our little Opel station wagon did not escape. It disappeared also, but somehow our driver Mohamed managed to retrieve it. When we got it back, it had been shot up with bullet holes and the upholstery was quite blood-stained.

There was intermittent shooting and firing of guns throughout the city. Our son John was at boarding school at this time and came home only on weekends. One morning, around Easter time, we discovered a bullet hole in the headboard of his bed. A stray bullet had pierced the wooden shutter and sliding window-door leading to the balcony of John's room, and found its way into the headboard. This was disturbing to all of us. Costa decided we should have a home base in the States. In 1973, he purchased six units in a new apartment complex on Gulfstream Avenue in Sarasota, Florida, called the Essex House. Essex House would not be completed until 1975, the year Penny was married. We moved into the penthouse at the Essex house that year, and it would become our State-side home until 1980.

Decorating the new apartment was a good project for me. I hired a decorator and enjoyed a fine relationship with her. We worked well together as a team. She took my ideas and ran with them. Also, she knew her way around Florida. I did not.

When Stephanie, not yet 17 years old, graduated high school from the Château Beau-Cedre in 1974, she was proficient in French. I felt she was too young to attend college in the States. In earlier years I had learned from a Baghdad friend of a fine bilingual secretarial school in downtown Geneva. She had sent her daughter there in the '60s, and Vivi had done well. So I said to Stephanie, "I suggest you go to a secretarial school, if that would please you; then you can go to a university in Florida." Stephanie agreed to attend the twelve-month bilingual secretarial course in Geneva. It worked out very well; she finished the year with honors.

In 1943, The National Pact, an unwritten agreement was put in place that laid the foundation for Lebanon to become an independent multi-cultural state. This Pact has shaped the country ever since.

We would have loved to continue living in Beirut, but when civil war broke out in 1975, it was no longer feasible. By mid-June the political situation was becoming more intense and difficult. Penny had graduated from St. Louis University in May with her degree in physical therapy. She was engaged to Tom Hicks, and was planning her wedding for July.

Stephanie had completed her bi-lingual secretarial course, so in June I flew to Geneva with Katherine to collect Stephanie and her belongings. We packed up her footlocker and left for the States. First we spent time with Mother in Kentucky. As Penny and Tom were planning their wedding in Indianapolis on July 25th, I made a few trips to Indianapolis to spend time with her. About mid-July, Costa arrived with John. The wedding took place as scheduled, and the newlyweds left for a month in England.

With the three younger children, Costa and I drove in two cars to Sarasota. Our apartments had been completed. We took up residence at the Essex House.

After we moved into the Essex House apartment, for a short time I seriously considered going to interior design school, as I had completed the three correspondence courses in interior design while in Beirut. The Ringling School of Art and Design, located in Sarasota, is a highly respected school. In the end, I decided not to apply. I did not believe it wise to be tied up for the better part of four years in Florida, and be separated from Costa most of that time.

In the fall of 1975, Stephanie began her freshman year at Florida Southern College in Lakeland. Katherine entered St. Mary's Academy in Owensboro, Kentucky as a ninth grader. I was heavily involved in getting them settled in, as well as getting our Florida apartments finished. I was up to my eyeballs with things to do.

After some business trips around the States that summer, Costa returned to the Middle East with John and enrolled him in the American School in Cairo. He was 12 years old at the time. I don't know what happened because I wasn't there, but in October, Costa called me and said he was sending John to the States. I went to Tampa to pick him up. His flight was from Kuwait to London, then a transfer flight to Tampa, but he wasn't on the flight. I panicked and wondered what in the world had happened to him. I drove an hour and a half back to Sarasota. It was midnight.

Getting home, I phoned Costa. "John didn't arrive. I don't know where he is, and the airline can't tell me anything." I was very disturbed, naturally.

Costa said, "I'll call you back." An hour later, after he'd made a few phone calls, he called to tell me John had missed the flight out of London, but he was being well taken care of; he would be on the next day's flight. The following day, I went back to Tampa and picked him up. Now all the children were in the States.

I enrolled John in Admiral Farragut Academy in St. Petersburg; he completed seventh and eighth grade there. He did well, although I believe he was not in love with the school. It was also during this time, after a number of months and numerous trips to the Immigration Office in Tampa, John at age 14 was finally sworn in and received his American citizenship. Fortunately, during that winter I was mostly in Florida.

In the early summer of 1977, John graduated eighth grade from Farragut. Mary and Jerry Mason, ex-Beirutis, and good friends, now living in St. Petersburg, came along with me for John's graduation.

John was often getting into some sort of mischief. It was never very serious, but Admiral Farragut Academy is a military school. The students wear uniforms and are under a strict code of conduct.

Once when coming back to Florida from Beirut, my mother arrived with John at the Tampa airport to pick me up. His arm was in a sling. It was shocking. He had been horsing around with some other boys and had run his arm through a glass door, requiring fourteen stitches.

In the fall of 1977, at the beginning of his Freshman year, John was expelled from Admiral Farragut. On this particular evening, Costa and I were at the Hilton Hotel in Athens entertaining twelve people at dinner. At around 9 p.m., the desk clerk came to us and said to Costa, "You have a phone call."

Costa left the table and took the call. It was Admiral Farragut calling to say we must come to St. Petersburg immediately and pick up John; they were not going to have him there any longer. John had stolen a dollar from one of the boys to buy ice cream and candy. We did get through dinner without anyone knowing our problem. As soon as possible my husband said to me, "Well, you are just going to have to go to the States."

I said, "No, *you* are going to the States." I had never spoken so sternly to Costa. Then I added, "and *you* are going tomorrow morning. *You* are going to Florida, and *you* are going to take care of this."

"But I don't have a ticket," he said.

"You will find one. You are going to the airport tomorrow morning." I was determined that he was going to take care of this issue. So he left Athens the next morning. With connections, it took another day for him to get to Sarasota and drive to St. Petersburg. He phoned me when he arrived. A week later, I arrived in Sarasota and went to see Col. Moriarity, John's advisor at Farragut. By then both Costa and John had left Florida. I always believed that had it been in Col. Moriarity's hands, things would have been different. John would have been sternly reprimanded but allowed to remain in school. As Costa used to say though, the powers that be would not allow that to happen. This was the fall of 1977.

In 1975, the same fall that John entered Farragut, Katherine began high school with the nuns in Owensboro, Kentucky. The summer that Elvis died, (1977) I picked her up to go back to Florida, and she announced to me that she wanted to become a nun. When I relayed this information to Costa, he was fit to be tied. Katherine did not return to Kentucky that fall. Instead, she was enrolled in Montverde Academy near Lakeland, Florida, where Stephanie was studying at Florida Southern College. When John was expelled in November 1977, I brought him to Montverde to be near Katherine. She was in her junior year and would finish high school in 1979, as salutatorian of her class. I was proud of her.

Katherine entered Simmons Women's College in Boston in 1979, and earned a degree in International Relations in 1983. She graduated again from Simmons in 1992, this time with a Nursing Degree.

Though not too happy at Montverde, John finished his freshman and sophomore years there. When Katherine graduated, I transferred him to Fryeburg Academy, a boys school in Fryeburg, Maine, located at the New Hampshire state line and near North Conway.

The headmaster of Fryeburg, Mr. True, was a fine man, and knew well how to handle boys. There were a few incidents—sneaking out to go to town, a block away, getting caught smoking, etc.—but for the most part John got along well and was happy there. He graduated high school the summer of 1981. Costa and I were both present. This was the only time that Costa was present for a graduation of any of his children.

Sometime in 1974, Costa was on a trip in Boston and went on to Scituate to visit our accountant, Wally Pyne. When he reached Wally's office, Wally said, "Costa, let's go up to North Conway for lunch. I have a young friend there who is building condominiums, just outside of town and he is looking for investors." Costa agreed, and off they went.

It is a two and a half hour drive from Boston, but they went for lunch. Aram, the developer, was really hurting for help. Costa said, "Okay, let's go to the bank and talk about this." When they walked into the North Conway Bank, Costa saw a man sitting and speaking to the manager.

Costa said, "Hi Wes, how are you?"

"Costa Halkias!"

"Wes Gleason!"

Wes and his wife Carrie had been our very close friends in Baghdad twenty years before. Their first child Scott was born in Baghdad a few weeks after our first son was born in Chicago. So, my goodness, here was someone from our Baghdad days. Costa had not seen him for all these years, and there he was sitting in this tiny bank in a small New Hampshire town. Now when in Boston with the girls, we often visit Scott and his wife.

Wally Pyne is the reason we ended up owning property in North Conway. My husband did go ahead and invest in Aram's project. He bought two units in the complex, one of which we kept for our own use; the second became a rental. For years, we spent parts of each summer as well as two or three weeks at Christmastime in North Conway. Costa never stayed the full time, but he came and went. Usually, I would stay for a month at a time, and the children would be there as much as possible. We had some great friends and enjoyed many happy times in North Conway. In the mid-1980's we sold those units. One friend from that time now lives in the Boston area, and we continue to stay in touch.

We now had a home in Florida, one in New Hampshire, the island house on Chios, an apartment in Beirut, and a villa in Kuwait. With all these places to look after, one day I told Costa, "We have too many places. I don't know where anything is!" Even though Costa was away from home a lot, we had friends in all the various places where we lived, and I was never lonely.

I helped Costa with the business as best I could. He wrote good letters, but he depended on me to polish them for him, so I edited and typed all his letters. I helped from home and sometimes from the office in Kuwait, but I was not with Costa in Kuwait on a continuous basis.

The Syrians entered and occupied Lebanon in 1975 and remained for twenty years, controlling and meddling in every facet of the government, including the Port of Beirut as well as the Airport. When war broke out in 1975, our company owned six of the duty-free shops at Beirut Airport. We had gold, watches, perfume, men's accessories, pens and luggage shops. (I have two watches purchased from our duty-free watch shop which I still wear.) Behind the Syrian army came many, many "important" Syrian business men, who took over the airport, including all the duty-free shops. They cleaned them out, along with the warehouse. They hauled all of the merchandise to Syria; we had nothing left but empty shelves. We were some of the big losers. Fortunately, however, we were able to retain our office and warehouses in the city. J. Rudolph & Co. continued to operate until 2007, at which time I closed the office for good.

We kept our Beirut apartment from 1968 until 1994, and sometimes Costa would use it when in Beirut. I stayed away from Lebanon from 1975 until 1982, only to return for a short period to have foot surgery.

Kuwait

By 1976, the situation in Beirut was going from bad to worse. We were spending our time back and forth between Florida, New Hampshire, Chios, and Kuwait. Though we kept the Beirut apartment, we had moved most of the necessities to our villa on Tyre Street in Kuwait. The Sheik of Kuwait had long ago built nineteen villas on a strip of land surrounding the Palace. These villas were available for rent, and Costa found the opportunity to rent one of them. It was a medium-size house with three bedrooms, along with all the other necessities. It was certainly pleasant enough, with a large garden. Costa hired a cook/houseboy as well as a gardener, and managed to make the garden quite beautiful.

We were not the owners but were allowed to renovate and make this villa livable to our satisfaction. I thought it would be fun to live in a pink house. "Why do you want a pink house?" Costa asked me. "I just do, " I said. So the house was painted and came to be known as the pink house on Tyre Street.

From the police department, Costa was offered a beautiful German Shepherd. The police had brought a number of these dogs into the country, planning to use them in their work. They never did and ended up giving them away. Costa was thrilled to receive this gift. The dog was about a year old, and Costa named him Rex.

Costa's Kuwati partner/sponsor from 1960 remained with him through the years. Even after Costa suffered a stroke, and until I liquidated the business in 2005, the son of the same sponsor had carried on. This sponsorship had been passed down from the father to the son about ten years before it ended.

Our Beirut office remained open and continued to limp along for more than a few years. The war had become of serious intensity, and Costa rarely traveled there. During this time the office was kept going by a secretary, a driver, and an office boy.

In October 1976, for our 25th wedding anniversary, we took an extended trip, combining business with pleasure. Costa rarely traveled anywhere unless it was business—except to Austria. He loved to cross-country ski, thus we made many trips to Austria through the years, both with the children, and to ski with friends who were wintering there. Of course our trips to Vienna were always special.

Our anniversary trip started in Kuwait, with a first stop in London. There we learned that Barbara Michon, Pierre's wife had died in a car accident six months earlier. Pierre and Barbara had stayed on in Baghdad after the Revolution in 1958. In early 1976, they had been driving in the countryside at night. A truck was parked on the side of the highway with no warning lights. Pierre hit the truck. He was an excellent driver, but could not swerve in time. One of the support rods of the truck rammed through their car, and Barbara died at the hospital a few hours later. After some years, Pierre took the children back to Toulouse in France. We never heard further from him.

From London, we flew to Copenhagen for a Sheaffer Convention where we remained for three days. (Sheaffer's headquarters were in Fort Madison, Iowa, southwest of Davenport on the Mississippi River. Of course Costa made many trips there through the years.)

From Copenhagen, we stopped over in Anchorage to refuel, en route to Tokyo. It was a long, long flight. From Tokyo we went on to Osaka. One of our representations in five or six countries of the Middle East was a Japanese luggage company called Ace Luggage. Costa, through the years, made a number of trips to Japan. The Ace people were delightful. The owner, Mr. Shinkawa, was a kind and gentle man and became very fond of my husband. Of course Costa had introduced Ace into most of the Arab countries and was deserving of their special treatment.

After a few days in Osaka, being feted and entertained, we left for Hong Kong to meet with a Sheaffer group as well as some Parker people. It was a lovely visit.

We transited Bangkok, and flew to Delhi, where we had one of the most ridiculous fights. Costa was always most generous with me. If there was something I wanted to buy or places I wanted to visit, he rarely said no to me. For the most part our years were good together, but there were also some difficult times. He was extremely jealous, to the point of being ridiculous.

In Delhi, one evening, we were sitting in the beautiful dining room of the Oberoi, one of the most fabulous hotels in the world, having dinner. I was wearing a lovely green Thai silk dress with matching green turban, and feeling at my best. There was a man sitting across the way having dinner alone, and out of nowhere, Costa said, "You are flirting with that man over there."

It was the farthest thing from my thoughts. I was *not* flirting with that man, had no idea who he was, nor cared, and wasn't even aware of him until Costa made his announcement. Our evening was spoiled. This is how I remember our time in Delhi. Living with Costa, I could never be sure of myself or of what was coming next.

I well remember going on to Agra to visit the Taj Mahal, one of the most beautiful sights you will ever see. Truly fabulous! From Delhi (Agra) we went to Katmandu. Our friends , the Wolles, (from Beirut as well as Baghdad days) had paid a visit there some years before and found it interesting. We found it a waste of time. The hotel had no proper dining room and we were obliged to eat at the so called restaurant down the street. It was early November, and the weather was cool, but sunny as I recall.

Katmandu was primitive and backward; there were few interesting things to do and see. After two days we were ready to leave. Good luck! The next plane scheduled out was not leaving for another three days. However, we were told we *must* visit such and such a village outside the city, near Bamian where the Russians had destroyed the famous Buddha statue that had been there for thousands of years. In this village, a young girl lived in a "palace" and she was "very holy." We must go and get a glimpse of her. This was to be an exciting event, and since we had nothing better to do, off we went. Upon finding the palace, and locating the window from which we would catch a glimpse of this "holy girl," we patiently waited the better part of an hour. No holy girl showed up; all we ended up seeing was a very dirty little town where dozens of monkeys frolicked about. So much for Katmandu.

Chios Renovation

Early in 1976, Costa decided that he would begin much-needed repairs to his house in Chios. The house was more than 300 years old, and any repair that had been done previously was *Rube Goldberg* style. We had been going there since 1959 and just made do each time. Costa engaged Mr. Thanos Kourtis, an Athens architect, and by November plans were complete. Work could now begin on this long and tedious undertaking.

The renovation was done in stages, and it took the better part of two years. Of course, Uncle Mike had passed away by this time. Demo had married Kiki, and they had two young boys, so the first part of the project was to create an apartment for Uncle Demo and his family on the ground floor level.

The next stage was to build two bedrooms and a bathroom over the barn as servants quarters. (That is where Costa and I stayed when we came to oversee the renovations during the winter months.) We did not have servants during this period. I helped Kiki with the cooking, and we ate with her and Uncle Demo.

In the main house, we added three bedrooms and repaired the large kitchen, adding all new cabinets and appliances brought from Athens. Before the renovation, we had been cooking on charcoal along with a little one-burner gas plate. This, Kiki knew how to manage, and with time I also learned. (One summer before the renovation, I had been in Chios, and upon going back to Athens, went to get my nails done. The manicurist saw the black under my nails, and asked, "*Where* have you been and what have you been doing? Look at your hands!")

I spent the winter of 1977-78 on Chios. Winters on the island are raw. The wind rushes down through the Aegean, between the mountains of Turkey and Chios. It can be cold, windy and icy. It never snows, but often there is sleet. We needed to dress warmly in jackets, coats and sweaters. I kept a portable heater in my room above the barn.

Costa came and went as the work progressed that winter. I was there 75 percent of the time. Greece is a man's world. If I gave an instruction to the contractor, he would say "Yes," and then walk away. Ninety percent of the time what I asked for did not get done. The issue would simply wait until Costa arrived and gave the same instruction. Then the project would get back on track again. This was very frustrating to me, but I had no choice. It was what it was.

We had ordered a number of pieces of knock-down unassembled furniture from the States, which (when Costa could be there) he proudly worked on and assembled himself. This was supplemented with purchases from the furniture stores, which I, many times, scoured in Athens, then shipped to Chios. We also patronized the few furniture shops in Chios Town, as well as special orders from some of the local carpenters. And we did, fully and to our satisfaction, furnish the house ourselves.

To ward off island fever, about once a month during that winter, I would fly to Athens for the a weekend or a few days. I would rent a car, visit friends, do some furniture shopping and maybe lunch at the Athens Hilton. Sometimes Costa and I would meet there and return to the island together.

Lest I forget, I was the proud seamstress of all the drapes in the house. My old portable second-hand Singer sewing machine which had been purchased in the early 1950s, was again put to good use. In Athens, I bought all the fabric and trimmings, and personally brought them to the island. It took much work and effort, as well as patience, but when finished I was happy and proud.

By mid-winter 1977-78, the house had become habitable. The ground floor TV room had a sofa as well as chairs and could sleep at least two persons. There was a full two-bed bedroom as well as a bathroom.

Off the bedroom was a room we called the cave. The walls of the house were extremely thick, at least two and a half feet, and when originally built, openings were provided for the inhabitants to shoot arrows from them to defend themselves. The cave had two of these openings. As if Greece had no wines, we brought wine from France. In

Egypt, we represented a very fine French wine company and stocked our cave with Calvet's best.

Up the stairs on the second floor was the living room with fireplace, dining room with small terrace, a family sitting area, kitchen, large bedroom and bathroom. The living room opened up onto a large terrace, off of which were two small rooms—one of which Costa used for an office and the other was mine. From the second floor terrace, an outside stairway led to the third floor and again, a large terrace. From this terrace, the entry was to a sitting room with fireplace, two bedrooms and a very large bathroom.

While renovating the Chios house, Kuwait became our home. Beirut was dangerous, uncomfortable, and unpleasant in too many respects. We spent a good amount of time traveling back and forth between Florida, New Hampshire, Kuwait, and Chios. Sometimes it was difficult, and even though I kept saying, "I don't know where anything is," I did get smart—at least part way—and eventually put together my Chios wardrobe. When on the island, we dressed very traditionally—no pants or shorts. I wore long dresses with sleeves and always covered my head with a scarf. The girls also wore dresses. My island clothes were washed, ironed, and hung in the closet; there they remained until we arrived the next time.

By the summer of 1978, the house was complete. A tennis court and a squash court had been built. Our designated flower garden was full of beautiful flowers. We could proudly say we were ready to receive family and friends—and did so many times—for however long any and all wished to remain. We were blessed with a cook, houseboy, and a maid. The houseboy served at table, as well as assisted the cook and maid. These three took care of all the housework. Happily, I was the gardener. We had a strict rule: no bathing suits, bare feet, or soiled clothing were allowed at the dining room table; everyone was to be clean and dressed for dinner.

Costa had originally hired the household help in Beirut and brought them to the island. The cook and houseboy (both Sudanese) were related to each other, and both were named Mohamed. We called the cook Big Mohamed and the houseboy was Young Mohamed. Big Mohamed spoke Greek and truly enjoyed the ouzo from our neighbor's factory. When as we often did entertain, he was happy to *entertain* with us. Young Mohamed was much more reserved than Big Mohamed.

All three of our hired help always dressed in uniforms. The Eritrean maid's uniform was white or pastel colors; the men wore black trousers and white jackets. The cook was of course in his chef's jacket. I purchased the white jackets and maid's wear in the States. All three, being the only blacks on the Island, became known as the *mavres*, which is the Greek word for blacks.

When I arrived back in Chios in May of 1978, Costa was there with the help and the house was in shipshape. Upon arrival, he called them out from the kitchen and said to me, "Madam, your staff." Everyone laughed.

In the coming years, I would usually go to Chios in May, around my birthday. Costa would gather up the servants from Cairo, Beirut, or wherever they were and bring them to the island. Big Mohamed would usually give Costa a scare at the airport, any airport, by wandering off at flight time. Somehow, he would always turn up, and Costa managed to get them to and from the Island in a timely order. Normally we spent June, July and part of August on the island, with Costa going and coming during those months.

One of those summers, I managed to get my hands on a high school English workbook. Thus, I decided that as long as both

Katherine and John were weak in English, we would have a one-hour morning session each day and work through this book. At 10 a.m. class opened, and we would work until 11 a.m.

"What?! Study?! We didn't come from half-way around the world to study English! We're here to play tennis, squash, go to the beach, roam around town, or sit at the port and watch the ships come and go." Both were firmly convinced that I was intent on torturing them with slow death to get through the English work book. We *did* get through it, they *did* learn at least something, but the entire process was like pulling teeth.

For the better part of the 1978 summer we entertained visitors, as we did many more summers to come. Even after the children were married, they came and brought the grandchildren. My mother visited Chios twice: the summer of 1978, and again in the summer of 1989.

Our many visitors would come from the States, Beirut, or England, and remain usually for ten days or two weeks. Each day after lunch, we would all load up in our little green Chevy car (I called it the Green Hornet), along with a taxi which had been hired for the duration and head for the beach. There were two beaches which we favored— Agia Fotia and Los Bay. Few tourists came to the island. For the most part, visitors were ex-patriots of Chios returning with their families for the summer months. Occasionally, one would see some backpackers on the ferry who had been tramping around Turkey and had decided to check out Chios.

One of our pleasures was at full moon, when I would prepare a picnic supper, (usually fried chicken, potato salad, etc.) load up just before dusk, and go off to Ayia Fotia Beach for a late swim and watch the full moon rise from over Turkey. At other times we would all gather on the top terrace to watch for the moonrise, then stay on looking up to the heavens trying to identify stars and constellations with Costa's telescope. The view of the Milky Way on the island was breathtaking.

Sometimes we would catch the ferry to Çeşme to spend the day. The trip involved showing your passport and passing through customs, a simple procedure. Upon arrival in Turkey, we would poke through the marketplace for an hour or so, then amble back to the port area to a little restaurant we came to know, sitting at the old wooden tables and chairs to eat *kufta* (meatballs) with fried potatoes and salad, as well as eggplant in some form. My, my, do the Turks know how to cook eggplant! Cats, lots of cats, would be under our feet waiting for their share.

Now and then, we would go to Izmir to shop and sightsee. After arriving in Çeşme, we would walk to the bus station to catch the bus which would take us the one and a half hour drive over the mountains to Izmir. Once, I thought we would never arrive. The driver kept stopping and leaving the bus to smoke a cigarette. Or was it pot? He was a rather wild driver and the road *is* mountainous!

Many Greeks, as well as various other nationalities, were still represented in Izmir even in the late 1900s. This remained so, in spite of the deliberate destruction of this thriving, gracious city in 1922, in an attempt to rid the city of as many foreigners as possible. The city was burned, and the people were literally running for their lives. Rescue ships arrived, but they were too few, and many people simply threw themselves into the sea to escape the fire and drowned. Mustafa Kemal Atatürk (also known as the Grey Wolf) took over Turkey at the end of the Ottoman Empire in 1923, after it gained independence.

When our children were old enough, they sometimes took the ferry alone to Çeşme for the day. Sitting around on the balcony in the evening, a daily routine, they'd say, "Daddo, can we go to Turkey tomorrow?" Costa would then hurry off to town—he would be gone a half hour, and return with the boat tickets for the next morning's ferry ride at 6:00 a.m.

After the house was restored, when people would talk about their yachts, Costa would say, "Chios is my yacht." He loved this house and garden with all his heart.

Chios before renovation

Chios after renovation

Boston

The summer that the Chios renovation was completed, we bought an old brownstone in Boston, and we went into partnership with Aram, the man with whom we invested in the North Conway condominiums. Costa and I were looking for a brownstone in Boston to develop into condominiums, and Aram located the building on Commonwealth Avenue in Back Bay. Winston Churchill once said, "Commonwealth Avenue in Boston is the most beautiful street in America." We found it quite lovely. The street on both sides, left, right and center, were lined for blocks with pink magnolias.

The property at 175 Commonwealth Avenue was called The Church of Jesus Christ, Inc.; it even had a plaque on the door stating this name. We purchased the building from Wesley Price, the man who preached there.

The project got off to a rocky start. Costa was financing the entire project, and he was convinced that Aram (who was operating as project manager) was wasteful and careless with money. So we halted the project and fired the contractor. I took over as project manager and hired a new contractor. After a total of two years, the building was ultimately finished and subdivided. We sold our place at Essex House in Florida and moved into the two top floors of 175 Commonwealth Avenue in 1980. The remaining three units were sold off at a respectable profit.

Upon graduation from Florida Southern College, Stephanie traveled with Costa for about nine months, primarily in the Middle East. During that time, she attended a Duty Free Symposium with us in the South of France. In the fall, she began a Masters Business Program at Tulane University in New Orleans, where she met her future husband, Randy Dalia.

Stephanie completed her MBA at Tulane in 1981. I drove from Boston to Kentucky to pick up my mother and step-father, then on to New Orleans to attend the Tulane graduation. We spent four interesting and pleasant days there. After graduation, Stephanie and her girlfriend Val took a cross-country driving trip before she began her employment in September at Chase Manhattan Bank in New York.

Stephanie and Randy were married on October 16, 1982, at the church of St. Thomas More in New York City. The morning wedding was beautiful—as was Stephanie—and the reception was held at the Waldorf Astoria, with an early reception in the Basildon Room. Afterwards lunch was served in the Jade Room, while we enjoyed the music of the Eddy Duchin Band—dancing of course—and oodles of Lanson Champagne.

John, Katherine, Me, Costa, Stephanie and Randy, 1982

Falmouth

One day Costa said, "I want to start shooting again." He loved shooting wild ducks and geese. Thus, in 1981, we bought an English Tudor in Falmouth, Maine, just north of Portland. The house was built in 1929 on four acres located next to the water. Although it needed quite a lot of repair, we handled it well and finished up a few months later.

Wanting to furnish this house in all-English furniture, I made a trip to Highpoint, North Carolina, where I bought and shipped a truckload of furniture to Falmouth. In Portland, I had made contact with an excellent and experienced decorator, John Houghton, who assisted me. The house turned out lovely. Especially beautiful was our dining room with the Queen Anne furniture—upholstery was light blue, the wallpaper with red birds on a cream background, and a red, blue and cream Kerman rug.

The problem was: *The house was haunted.* Only a few weeks before moving in, a neighbor said to me, "You know, this house is haunted." He was right. The man who had built it had committed suicide in the attic, just a year or so after the big financial crash of 1929. I was very uncomfortable, and as time went on, I became more and more miserable. Costa was rarely with me, spending most of his time in the Middle East. Anyway, he was never bothered by ghosts. Instead, he would say, "When I am here I sleep so well!" But me, I could hear noises in the attic. One night I started upstairs. It was Christmastime; all the children were home. As I mounted the steps, I heard running down the hallway. Everyone except me was downstairs. Over the garage, from the main part of the house, I went to the wing of servants' rooms, looked about—there was nothing.

We had a fine couple who lived as caretakers next to the main house. Their quarters were an extension from a breezeway and built over a small garage and garden room. Mr. Edsel took care of the grounds, mowed the grass, kept wood in place for the five fireplaces, and drank lots of beer. He wasn't a bad person, just a bit on the slow side, and could never have survived without Mrs. Edsel. (He did not.)

Mrs. Edsel was a great lady. She decorated the house so beautifully for Christmas, was a great cook, and sewed like a professional. She was the *best* of housekeepers: always pleasant and smiling, never complaining nor asking what needed to be done. She just did it! Their names were Merton and Gertrude Edsel—Mert and Gert. He always referred to her as Gert, but she called him Mr. Edsel, never referring to him as Mert.

Once I discovered an odor in Costa's closet, while rearranging his clothing. I went downstairs to get Mrs. Edsel. "Mrs. Edsel, come upstairs with me."

"What is it?" she asked.

"Come with me," I said. In Costa's bedroom, I opened the closet door and said, "What does that smell like?"

"A dead body," she said.

Well, that was nearing the end for me.

While we had Falmouth, John was living there and going to school in Maine. He had graduated from Fryeburg, and he had been given a used car, not the best, but good enough for a first car. So, one day, it was a few days before I returned from the Middle East, he decided to *borrow* Mr. Edsel's truck for some reason or other, without his permission of course, and was gone a few hours. Mr. Edsel never forgave John for this. John was often doing such things. He'd pick up someone's coffee cup from the table and drink it. Two or three hours later he would be back with some flowers or a box of chocolates for that person. "What difference did it make?" he would say. Same with Mr. Edsel's truck. He didn't harm the truck, only borrowed it. Sometimes I'd think, *John, whatever is wrong with you?*

Brian, our first grandchild who was born in 1978, spent six weeks with us in Falmouth when he was four years old. Penny and Tom had recently suffered the death of their second son, Stephen, in Saudi Arabia, and had separated. Penny left Tom in Saudi Arabia, and returned with Brian to the States. Shortly after her return however, she was given the opportunity to return for a six-week work period at the King Feisal Hospital in Riyadh as a physical therapist. Brian remained with me during that time. We got along well except for one day when I found him trying to saw the leg off the kitchen table with a toy saw he had been given for Christmas. I was upset and swatted his backside a few times, but Mrs. Edsel came to his rescue.

I did not at all like living in a house of ghosts, so every week or ten days I would drive to Boston for the day, perhaps to meet a friend, have lunch and shop a bit. Finally I told Costa, "We must sell Falmouth. I cannot remain here." Since he was seldom there with us, he did not disagree with me. We brought in an auctioneer and held the auction on the lawn. Everything went; we kept nothing of that house. Surely we lost money, but I neither wanted nor did I keep anything associated with it. I just wanted to be done with the ghosts!

The Edsels were disappointed when I told them we were leaving, and I did feel bad for them. They, however, found work nearby in Falmouth with good people. It was not solely living in the haunted house that was bothering me. I knew that I had to spend more time with my husband, and it was not easy to do so living in Falmouth, Maine.

The children were grown, and Costa was still traveling far and wide. I detected signs that he wasn't happy with me because I was not with him, and he needed my help in the business. He was expanding, and needed me close by. It was always a great disappointment to Costa that none of his children chose to became part of his business world.

It isn't good for any marriage—couples spending too much time apart—and I knew that if Costa found someone else to share his life with, I would be the loser. Buying a house in Maine was nonsense from the start. It was time to leave.

Unfortunately, we had sold the condominium on Commonwealth Avenue, so when we did go back to Boston, we rented a place downtown at The Devonshire until we found the right place to buy.

In the fall of 1982, I developed a neuroma in a toe on my right foot, a painful condition affecting my ability to walk. I only wanted to be cared for in Beirut. Our family doctor was still there, and I knew the surgeon I wanted to perform the surgery. Costa brought the servants, opened up the house, and I was off to the hospital. This was during some of the really bad days of the war.

The surgery was performed on the fifth floor of the Fouad Khoury Hospital. There was a generator for the operating room, but no electricity for the lift. Our houseboy and the driver, another Mohamed, carried me post-surgery down the five floors on a chair to the car and took me home where the electricity worked just fine. I remained three weeks in Beirut until my foot healed well enough to travel.

Things continued to go from bad to worse in Lebanon. By 1983 hundreds of innocent people were dying, as well as being kidnapped. Truck bombers killed 241 American servicemen in the Marines' barracks next to the Beirut airport. An obscure group called the Islamic Jihad claimed responsibility for this bombing. Times were really bad. It was war.

In the fall of 1984, we put a contract on the apartment at 360 Beacon Street in Boston and, after some renovations, moved in the spring of 1985. As we had retained in storage, all the furniture from 175 Commonwealth Avenue, it was used to furnish the Beacon Street apartment. We were now splitting our time between Cairo, Kuwait, Boston, and North Conway, as well as Chios.

Cyprus

The last school John attended in his youth was the American University of Cairo (AUC), but that didn't work out. We had opened an office in Larnaca on the Island of Cyprus, in partnership with an Englishman named Chris Harrison. We were deeply into the cigarette transit business. Chris took John in, and he worked in that office for three years. Even though Costa was financing this entire operation, Chris was the boss.

After the three years, John said, "I am just not going to do this any longer." Chris was living high on the hog, at our expense, and making many mistakes. Looking back, I expect John became aware of much more than he ever let us know. He quit the job and left Cyprus.

Earlier, we had purchased quite a lovely little house in Larnaca, on a quiet neighborhood street, believing John would stay on and live there. Though not a large house, it was nice—typical Mediterranean. There were three bedrooms and two bathrooms upstairs. The downstairs consisted of a sitting room, office with fireplace, guest bathroom, dining room and large kitchen. There were two lovely terraces and a large garden. There were also two servants' rooms and a bath. I gave the larger bedroom to Costa, the medium one was for John and I took the smaller one. My bedroom, (something I had always wanted to do) I dared to decorate in purples, lavender and pink—my color scheme.

When John left Larnaca, we were ready to sell the house, including all the furniture, John's car and his wind surfer. Costa soon arrived in Larnaca, prepared to put the house on the market. As he was putting the key in the gate to enter, an English couple was driving by. They were looking for a house to buy and stopped to speak to him. He invited them in, offered them wine, and after visiting for an hour or so (and two bottles of wine), they were ready to buy the house, windsurfer, car and all. They did so, and I might say, at a very nice price.

After John left Cyprus, Costa took him to the Kuwait office to work. John did not care for the manager running the Kuwait office; neither did I. He did spent a year there, but when Katherine was married in Boston on April 30, 1988, he came for the wedding and refused to go back to Kuwait—as well as anywhere else in the Middle East.

The Cairo Duty Free Years

In 1986, when the Cairo Airport opened up Terminal Two, with seven boarding gates which that were to primarily service European, Gulf, and Far East Airlines, the duty-free shops were put out for bid. Our company International Tax Free Company, or INTAFREE, won the bid. Costa based his business plan on servicing these airlines when he bid on the shops. Cigarettes, liquor, watches, luggage, gold, silver, jewelry, as well as locally produced gift items, such as caftans, papyrus, and alabaster are big purchases for passengers traveling internationally on non-Arab/Muslim countries, but are not necessarily desirable for passengers on the Arab airlines. In order to be successful, it was imperative that the great majority of traffic coming through Terminal Two be non-Arab airlines.

Our company, J. Rudolph & Co, partnered with the Brazilian company BRASIF which created International Tax Free Company or INTAFREE, the Egyptian company. Costa decided he wanted me to become more involved. To begin with, I was supposed to have a small office within the Brazilian office in London. Upon arriving in London, nothing worked out as had been promised or planned. In the main office, I was put off in a corner, and all but completely ignored. Before going, Costa said, "I want you to be my eyes and ears." Well, the partnership made sure that I would *see no evil, hear no evil, or speak no evil*. Once, when one of the two Brazilian owners arrived in London, I was not allowed to see him. After five months of being ignored, I left for Cairo.

In the 1970s when Costa initially opened up an office in Cairo, it was much to my disappointment. Figuratively, I hit the ceiling—I really did. (He also did business in Alexandria, but we never maintained an office there.) Costa went into partnership with Victor, a Lebanese-Egyptian who had been born in Egypt. The children loved him. He was a great entertainer, but he was worthless in the business world. In a nutshell, he never, ever worked. He was lazy and needed a keeper to survive. He was a great talker, smoker, and drinker. Likeable, but useless. He did, however, have some reasonable contacts in Egypt. Costa tolerated him because that was how he could get the Egyptian business on line in the 1970s. Victor passed away in 1981.

A short time after opening the office in Cairo, Costa established an office and warehouse facilities in Port Said. Port Said is located on the Mediterranean at the mouth of the Suez Canal, two and a half hours by car, northeast of Cairo. The port is a Free Zone, and upon leaving the city, there are custom controls. If a purchase of value is made, customs are charged before entering Egypt, so to speak.

Costa did not involve me in the setting up of these businesses in Egypt because he knew how I felt. Sometimes he felt the same way I did—but it didn't stop him.

> October 10, 1979
> Athens
> Dearest Jessie:
> Port Said is a Den of Thieves. The manager whom we thought above all was honest was on the take. I'm trying to clean it up. It is not going to be easy.
> We have to fight to get things moving.

My intuition told me to not become involved in Egypt. I did not trust the Egyptians. I had heard enough stories from others, mostly hearsay, but there must be some truth to what one hears if heard often enough over the years.

One story supposedly took place in the early 1980s. Toyota products were selling well in Egypt. One of the President's sons wanted the Toyota Agency. There were others who had held the Toyota dealership for years, but when the son said to his father, "I want the Toyota Agency," his father said, "Of course," and simply cancelled the dealership, confiscated the inventory from these people, and gave it to his son. The rightful owners received nothing.

This story, I heard at the very start of the duty-free operation at Terminal Two in the Cairo airport, and I believed it.

Another story involved the First Lady of Egypt at the time. The public schools in Egypt are truly bad. Buildings are rundown, no heat in winter, and certainly no air conditioning in summer. The students learn little or nothing. The First Lady decided she would host a reception outside of one of the schools to demonstrate how much better the schools are under her husband's rule. Instead of renovating or cleaning up the building, she had a new façade—a wall—built in front of the school, and held the reception outside the wall. Nothing had been done to improve the interior of the building, and no guests were allowed inside. It was only a façade. A sham. These were the kinds of things one would hear about the Egyptian government. There were laws, but they applied only to certain people.

Because Costa was unable to locate an Egyptian company that was capable of promoting the airport shops, he partnered with the two Brazilians. I do not know how he came to know them. Perhaps they met because of the duty free shops we previously had in Lebanon. It did not matter. My husband was not Egyptian, but the company, INTAFREE, was set up as an Egyptian company.

The two Brazilians were experts in the duty free business. They maintained an office in London, staffed by experts. These experts had been involved deeply in the creation of the duty-free shops at Heathrow Airport. Jack Neema, from their London office, was designated as Project Manager, and C. J. Halkias and the Brazilians were the owners.

This was a large operation—the shops numbered 26. We had more than 60 employees on 24-hour duty, and our monthly rent was $125,000.

Costa and I purchased a two-story, 8,000 square foot apartment near the airport to be our home base while running the shops. It was called a *villa* and consisted of two levels, the eighth and ninth floor, in a large apartment building. I was responsible for decorating it. With great difficulty, I managed to do so, and it did turn out beautifully.

After about six months, when the shops were up and running, the Cairo Airport Authority (CAA) along with EgyptAir, the Egyptian airline, changed the economics of the arriving flights into the country. It became primarily Arab airlines arriving through Terminal Two. Costa tried everything possible, but the CAA refused to follow the original plan. It was an extremely difficult time. We hung on for another six months, even after it seemed as though we were not going to make it. It was, to say the least, extremely draining. We were at the airport daily. Both Costa and Jack Neema were doing their best to keep the project going.

Whether the Egyptians made this change intentionally in an effort to break us, or for other reasons, we never knew. We did, however, know immediately that EgyptAir and the CAA took charge of the duty-free area to run for themselves. They stole all the improvements and there were many made to the area, along with millions of dollars of merchandise. It became a ready-made profit center for the Egyptians, but a fast track to failure for us.

After we were forced out, the CAA may have brought back the European and Far East Airlines to Terminal Two—I do not know. Before starting the shops, Costa and partners had figured it would take a year to 18 months to begin making money. We went broke before we got started.

Costa had taken out a loan on our home through an Egyptian lawyer. The CAA was pressing us hard for the rent, enormous as it was, and the employees needed to be paid. Later I discovered this Egyptian lawyer was charging 36 % interest on the loan! The duty-free shops were to become our greatest financial loss.

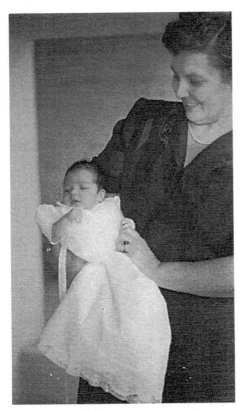

My mother with Penny, 1953

A Year of Losses

Summer was in her heart when she died, still believing she was young.

Anonymous

FAX

Feb 28, 1990

Paducah to C.J. Halkias, Larnica, Palm
Beach Hotel, Room 227

I have your two faxes of today. There
is so much going on here. Somebody in and
out all the time. Mother is very low.
There are many things to be decided and
done. It is a really emotional time and
things were really bad yesterday.

Today I am hiring nighttime help. She
is no longer capable of handling herself
during the night. We believe she has
reached the final stages of her illness.
She wanted you yesterday. We have started
to do the final arrangements for her. I
am very sad.

Yours with love, Jessie

FAX

March 3, 1990

Puducah

Dearest Costa:

It seems that Mother has only a few
hours left. Can you come on here right
away?

I will phone you early tomorrow
morning.

All my love,
Jessie

Mother died on Saturday, March 10, 1990, three weeks after her
82nd birthday. Costa had arrived a few days before her death. Her
funeral was held on March 12th at Bethlehem Church, and she was
buried in the cemetery next to my father, who had died fifty years earlier.

Our trip around the world was planned to begin April 1st. From Kentucky, we flew directly to Athens. I was constantly in tears. My mother was gone! After a few days in Athens, we went on to Kuwait, where the trip began. The first stop was Dubai, then onwards to Singapore, with a stop in Bangkok. We had three days of hot and muggy weather in Singapore. Then we went to Hong Kong for two days before flying to Osaka. Here I felt ill and unable to attend any of the functions that had been arranged for us.

From Osaka, we traveled to Hawaii where we spent three nice days visiting with Jean and Jim Gallo, a retired Marine Colonel. We had been friends and neighbors in Beirut. From Hawaii, we flew to Los Angeles for overnight and a day before leaving for Denver, our next stop. Checking in at the Brown Palace, I went directly to bed and remained there for three days.

It was early summer of 1990, in Chios when Costa said to our good neighbor, Rudy Halkussi, "I think I am going to sell this house. Do you know anyone who might want to buy it?" Rudy said, "I may." Costa and Rudy had known each other for *donkey's years*, as the English would say.

Long before this, Costa told me that if anything happened to him, I would have a very difficult time, if not impossible, to sell the property, that I would never get through it, and would die trying. Somehow the deed had been recorded or was mixed up with Turkey. The property had been purchased in 1938 from Mr. Perthwaite, an Englishman who lived in Izmir, so when the time came to sell, Costa was obliged to go to Izmir in search of records before he could finalize the sale. It was concluded in November, 1990.

Costa was right. I could have never been able to dispose of the property trying to get through the channels with my limited Greek. I could bargain for bread or coffee, and vegetables, but that was about all.

One particular evening, a short time later, Costa was away, perhaps in Athens, and I had gone to bed. At about 10 p.m. I heard the front gate open. Our bedroom was just off the living room which overlooked the courtyard. I went out to see who might be there. It was Rudy and he was calling in Greek, "Costa, Costa, pou issa?" (Where are you?)

From the window, I called, "Ah, Rudy."

"Ah Jessie μου, (my Jessie) where's Costa?"

"He's in Athens, but is coming back tomorrow."

"I have somebody who wants to buy the house. Not just interested, not just wants to look at it; he wants to buy it!" he said.

"He will be on the ten o'clock flight tomorrow morning." I said.

"Okay, have him call me or I'll pass by." Rudy passed by our house every day on his way to town.

Upon his arrival from Athens, Costa met with Rudy, and that afternoon, Rudy showed up with a young man named Mathew Los. Some years earlier, Mathew had spent time playing tennis with John. We remembered him. Driving by the house one day, he stopped and asked if he could play tennis on our court. Of course we invited him in, and John was delighted to have a new tennis partner.

Costa, Rudy, and Mathew went for a stroll around the garden and all the grounds. Shortly they returned to sit together on the terrace. I remained with them. The men spoke and drank wine. Soon Mathew said, "I think I will take this house." There was no bargaining on price. Costa had named the price and Mathew agreed to pay it.

Finally, I spoke, "Mathew, wouldn't you like to look at the rest of the house?"

"No, it's okay."

Although I had not met Christine, his wife, I said, "What about Christine? Wouldn't you like her to see the house before you decide?"

"No, it's okay. She will like it."

The decision had been made.

After about two weeks, still in the summer, Mathew phoned from Athens to say that he wanted to bring Christine to see the house. Although born in Canada, Mathew's parents were originally from Chios. Mathew and Christine lived in Athens part time and Canada part time.

To facilitate Christine's visit, inasmuch as we were selling everything, I had made a long list of all the furniture and household items. When I showed her the list as we walked through the house, she hardly looked at it and seemed to be pleased with everything she saw. When I asked her would she like to see such and such, her answer was, "No, it's okay." Everything was "Okay."

Actually, I was rather disappointed that she paid little or no attention to my list as I had made a great effort getting it together. Well and good. Whatever Mathew decided, that was okay.

Within a week, we packed our few personal belongings, loaded them in our little car, boarded the ship and sailed to Athens where we settled into our small apartment in Voula.

Selling the house in Chios was spiritually a great loss for Costa, as well as the children and me. There is no longer anything or any connection for us in Greece. Twenty-five years later, I still feel the void in my life from that August day in 1990.

Meanwhile, at the beginning of August 1990, Saddam Hussein invaded Kuwait, and we suffered another loss. We were robbed of about $1.5 million in merchandise and were only able to recover less than a million. This was the same year we lost Mother, sold our home in Chios, and lost *everything* at the Cairo Airport.

Things had gone from bad to worse in Cairo. I was in Boston and Costa was phoning me daily. It was just before Christmas of 1990 when he called and said, "The hammer has landed." He had gone to the Airport, but was not allowed to enter. The shops were closed and walled off. All our merchandise had been confiscated. Jack Neema had left the night before in the middle of the night. The Brazilians had simply floated away—Costa was left holding the bag. Not just banned from the airport, he was detained and forbidden to leave Egypt. Only in June the following year, 1991, did he manage to travel out of Egypt.

After we lost our home and furnishings, we rented a small furnished apartment in Cairo, while Costa desperately began trying to recover compensation from the Airport or Cairo Airport Authority (CAA). Fortunately, the Egyptian government never touched our other businesses in the country. Both the Cairo and Port Said offices were operating under the name of J. Rudolph & Co, and those operations were left intact.

INTAFREE had as much as $12 million invested in merchandise and infrastructure, but we also lost $40 million in potential revenue had we continued to operate the shops with our Brazilian partners.

A number of times Costa and I went to the American Embassy in Cairo asking for assistance. Ambassador Pelletreau was understanding and pleasant always, but basically offered nothing. One of the last times we paid a visit to the Embassy, the Ambassador was out of town. We met with the Counselor of Embassy. In the meeting with the Counselor, Costa again went through his story, pleading his case. The Counselor's reply was "What do you want us to do? Swat a fly on the wall with an intercontinental ballistic missile?" So much for help from the U.S. Government!

Within five minutes, we were out of there. Costa and I were both livid. I do not know if he went back to the Embassy again, but I do know they did *nothing* for us. This is how the American government treats expatriates doing international business. A few years later, when I met Ambassador Pelletreau at a funeral in Washington, I reminded him of the story of his Counselor. There was no response. Just a smile. He *was* an Ambassador.

Costa struggled for more than seven years to find a way to recover, at least partial reparations, from this fiasco. Our court case with the CAA went nowhere. We failed to recover a cent for the merchandise confiscated by them. Nothing ever came of it. All simply evaporated.

Washington D.C

In 1993, we sold our 360 Beacon Street home in Boston and moved to Washington, D.C. Costa felt that if we were nearer to Government and international lawyers, he would have a better chance with the Cairo court case. He tried to work through the World Bank, as well as a number of other international organizations in an effort to solve this Egyptian debacle and hopefully receive some degree of reparations. It was all in vain, unfortunately. We spent thousands of dollars, but all his desperate endeavors came to naught. At one point, Costa had brought an international lawyer from Washington to Cairo, along with his wife, but all to no avail. Nothing was ever accomplished, not an iota.

The Egyptians were not only a den of thieves, but bald-faced liars as far as we were concerned.

During our time in Washington, Costa requested that Ron Brown, Secretary of Commerce under the Clinton administration, write a letter to Mubarak pleading our case. We did receive a copy of the letter, but later learned it was never signed *or* sent. I found the original of this letter, along with a statement saying it was never sent. That's Washington for you. You are on your own!

We had suffered downturns before: Baghdad in 1958: Beirut in 1974-75, and Kuwait in 1990, but the Egypt duty-free loss was the one that broke Costa's spirit, as well as his health. In later years, I realized that it was only our son John who truly understood the extent of my anger and bitterness toward Egypt.

For more than twelve years we had traveled to Cannes, in the south of France, during the month of October. First it was to keep in touch with contacts for the duty free business. Secondly, it was to celebrate our October wedding anniversary. However, in the fall of 1998, Costa said, "We are not going to Cannes this year." I asked if we could go to Vienna instead. Having been there a number of times through the years, we always enjoyed it immensely. So this year, we went for the final and last time. We stayed at the Sacher Hotel. It doesn't get better than this. Also we did attend an opera, the name of it I have long forgotten, enjoyed delicious food, and wonderful coffee, but did little else. Costa was not interested in doing much of anything; he was depressed. He would sit for hours reading the newspaper, or doing and saying nothing.

In November, a month after the Vienna trip, while I was in Cairo and he was in Kuwait, he suffered a small stroke. I believe he was paralyzed momentarily, perhaps his speech was temporarily affected, but it soon corrected itself. Within a few days he left for Beirut. He called his cousin Jacob. Being a doctor, Jacob insisted that Costa come with him to the American University of Beirut Medical Center. They met there and Costa was examined. He told the doctors, "I need to go to the bank." The doctors told him he must return immediately after his errand to the bank. But Costa had no intention of returning to the hospital. He left, did not go to the bank, (he had no need of going to the bank) and never returned. Had he returned for treatment, he may not have suffered the stroke that turned him into an invalid for the last six years and eight months of his life. What I understand now so clearly (hindsight of course) is this: He lived his life the only way he knew: *his way*.

> *It matters not how strait the gate,*
> *How charged with punishment the scroll;*
> *I am the Master of my fate:*
> *I am the Captain of my soul.*

From *Invictus* by William Ernest Henley

Part IV

When you are sorrowful, look again in your heart, and you shall see that in truth you are weeping for that which had been your delight.

Kahlil Gibran

With Costa, Khalid and other business acquaintances at Monte Carlo, 1972

Christmas with Costa, circa 1985

A Beirut Reunion at the Prime Rib on K Street in Washington D.C. with the
Crouchleys and the Chellmans, circa 1995

235

Having fun with Roberta McCain on the roof top patio of our
Washington D.C. apartment, circa 1996

Yvonne Rodler and me at Roberta McCain's 100th birthday party, 2011

Beginning of the End

In late February 1999, we traveled to California to celebrate Costa's 76th birthday with friends in Los Angeles. Remaining there for three days, (with a side trip to San Diego to visit our old Baghdad and Cairo friends, the Barrows) we returned to Washington. The next two days were spent readying ourselves and repacking for the trip to New York where we were invited for the celebration of the 70th birthday of Bill Polk, one of Costa's dearest friends. We took the train, and since neither of us had been on Amtrak before, this was a new experience. We arrived at noon on Friday and checked into the New York Athletic Club where Randy had kindly reserved a suite for us. All was well.

237

The following early evening, we were in our rooms readying ourselves for Bill's party. I was in the bedroom dressing and Costa, who was almost ready, was in the sitting room putting on his cuff links. I was only partially dressed when I noticed how quiet it was in the other room. Going to the door and looking around, I did not see him.

"Where are you?" I asked. Then I realized he was on the floor next to the window and trying to speak.

When I reached him, he said, "Help me up."

I tried, but could not. He was dead weight. Immediately I realized he had had a stroke. Phoning the desk, I asked for help, telling them my husband had collapsed. In moments, two men were there getting him up. The ambulance arrived, and he was taken to St. Luke's Roosevelt Hospital. There he remained for a month.

When Costa suffered this stroke, my world was shattered. I was in total shock and didn't know what to do or where to turn next. Only to a certain extent did I know what was *out there* in the Middle East, and thought, *somebody is going to need to take care of all these things.* Costa had always been in charge; I was merely an assistant. There was so very much I did not know or understand about the businesses. *What am I going to do now?*

As they lived in Connecticut and nearest to New York, I immediately phoned Stephanie and Randy. They arrived at the hospital as quickly as they could after making arrangements for a sitter to come in and be with the children. It was to be a long night. Next I phoned Penny in Grand Rapids, then Katherine and John in Boston. All three arrived the following day. Penny was unemployed at the time, and she remained the entire month with me in New York while Costa was at St. Luke's Roosevelt. Stephanie, Katherine and John came and went as often as they possibly could. They had their work and children to attend to.

The day following the stroke I phoned Jack Pyne, our accountant and financial advisor. He arrived early the next day. By that time Penny's husband Terry had arrived from Grand Rapids. All the family was present.

We held a family meeting. Jack was in charge. My children have known Jack most of their lives and have always liked and highly respected him.

During the meeting, both Randy and Terry generously volunteered to leave their jobs and assist me through the forthcoming and difficult period, which obviously lay ahead of me. Neither of them, nor I, could have imagined that it would be more than six years before these problems could be fully resolved—satisfactorily and/or unsatisfactorily.

Jack Pyne is a large, tall, robust man, knowledgeable and kind. At last he had heard enough. Jack has been around a lot longer than any of my children or their spouses. After about two hours, he told them, "You, and you, and you can say whatever you want, anyone of you, but in the end, it will be Jessie, your mother, who will decide what she must do. She will have the final say on how this will be handled."

I had not spoken a word, but Jack's words killed the conversation. I then thanked both Randy and Terry, but refused their offers. There was no way I was going to have either of my sons-in-law jeopardize his future by quitting his job and trying to take over liquidation and the handling of Costa's affairs, in countries which they knew little or nothing about. Costa would not have wished it this way. Besides, neither of them had any real knowledge of Costa's business. I had spent most of my life assisting him, then, even I knew only a fraction of what was going on. What could *they* know?

To both Randy and Terry, I said, "Thank you very much; I don't think so. I do not believe it would work. You should not quit your jobs for my sake." Soon we adjourned for lunch. This was a task which I needed to handle myself. And I did so. I did it my way.

After a month in St. Luke's Roosevelt Hospital, Costa wanted to go to Massachusetts General in Boston. In the beginning, I listened to him as to what he wanted to do or where he wanted to be. We took him by ambulance to Mass General. He believed they could make him well again; they would fix everything. So we went to Boston, but they could not help him. His entire left side was paralyzed. He could still speak, but his speech was slow, and although we didn't know then, he was never to walk nor have use of his left side again. We still clung to the hope for at least partial recovery. Thus, we brought him to Boston by ambulance with a wild young woman at the wheel who exceeded the speed limit every chance she got. Despite the wild ride, we arrived safely at Massachusetts General where Costa remained in therapy for six weeks.

At Mass General, they were going to teach him to write checks, pay bills, and cook. Ridiculous! He never improved one iota. Instead he slowly and gradually deteriorated.

While Costa was trying to recover, impossible as it would be, in Boston, I took my first trip alone to the Middle East since the onset of his illness. This was my first attempt to begin the process of finding out what was necessary to begin this long and tedious undertaking of winding down his business affairs.

While I was gone, Costa asked our son John to take him back home to our Washington apartment. This apartment, located in an older and wonderful building, did not have doorways and bathrooms capable of accommodating a wheelchair. John put his father in the car and drove him back to Washington. Somehow they managed in the apartment for about a week before John brought him back to Boston. I only learned of this trip when I returned to the States a few weeks later.

After Mass General, we moved Costa to Beaumont, a nursing home in Natick, a few miles west of Boston and a facility located quite near Katherine's home. Being in the Boston area, it was reasonably convenient for both Katherine and John to visit their father often, and they did so. Both were as helpful as they could be, considering they had their job obligations plus Katherine had three young sons. Stephanie in Connecticut, too, with four young children and her family obligations visited as often as she could. Beaumont was a really fine nursing home. However, Costa still wanted to return to Washington.

John would bring Costa all manner of articles and newspapers to read. I do not know if he learned about it through an article, or if he saw it on the television. In any case, Costa decided that the National Institute of Health (NIH) in Washington could do wonders for him. We packed up and returned to Washington. Costa's aide, John Asamoah from Ghana, was excellent with him, but the doctor assigned to us at NIH was a first class fool. He would have Costa, John, and me sit around in a circle with the lights off and ask us to remain silent. Then he would say, "John [Asamoah] is the key to Costa's recovery." We went through this nonsense a number of times over a period of about three weeks. This doctor did not one particle of good for my husband. He was a complete fraud as far as I was concerned.

On my final visit to NIH, the doctor said something which caused me to explode. In a stern manner he retorted, "You leave now."

I left *now*, went outside, sat on a chair and cried. I thought to myself, *Well fella, you will not see us again!*

It was not possible for Costa to live in our Washington apartment, Mass General did him no good, and NIH was useless. I was lost and hardly knew where to turn. Shortly, I decided to rent a two-story, wheel-chair-accessible house in Alexandria where we set up Costa's bedroom on the first floor. We had the Eritrean maid with us, and I hired a second aide so that he had help both day and night. This worked out reasonably well for a short time, but each time I traveled, it seemed that a crises would occur with Costa. The maid or aides would phone Penny in Michigan. She would leave immediately, making the 900-mile drive to Alexandria. After some months, and numerous trips, this was becoming a hardship on her. She and I both decided there needed to be another solution. Besides the expense of the maid and two aides, the situation was becoming impossible.

Finally, Penny said, "Mommy, maybe Daddo should come to Michigan and stay with me." It was decided. Penny and Terry took Costa, along with his aide John Asamoah, to Michigan, much against his will. At the time I was in Cairo. When returning to Alexandria, I gave up the rental house and sold much of our furniture which felt like half my life.

We had been in Washington since 1993. Our home on Connecticut Avenue was spacious, comfortable, and beautiful. We, and sometimes only I, did lots of entertaining, giving great parties for lovely people. Most were old friends we had known from the Middle East. For me, the highlight of the year, was our black-tie Christmas Party. Entertaining was easy. Our Eritrean maid was always with us, and a wonderful serving man Juan was ever available to help. He would also bring extra help if needed. It was truly a grand time; I loved being and living in Washington. I put our lovely Washington home on the market. It did sell rather quickly which was a blessing.

The arrangement in Michigan worked well for a short time, but it soon became a strain on both Penny and Terry. It seemed that since Costa was going to be indefinitely in Michigan, it would be best to put him in a nursing home—the best we could find. John Asamoah remained with Costa in Michigan for about a year, but then traveled to Ghana and never returned.

Being a physical therapist and knowing the area well, Penny and I investigated a number of nursing homes. Returning to Penny's house, I sat down with Costa and told him, "You are going to need to move. We'll find you a really good nursing home, and you will go there." He did not object. He, too, could feel that his presence was too difficult for Penny and Terry.

In the meantime, I rented a small apartment in downtown Grand Rapids where I moved my remaining furniture and took up residence.

I felt very comfortable moving Costa to the nursing home. He was always a good sleeper, and I felt satisfied leaving the staff in charge of him during the night. He never complained, ever, even once, about the night staff, but *would* have if they were not doing their duties. Now that John Asamoah was gone, I hired two young Sudanese men who were nursing students. They would take turns spending 12-hour days with Costa. Both William and Kuol were very good to Costa.

Costa never complained about his condition. The nursing home was costly—more than $15,000 per month—but we did what we needed to do. He would have done no less for me! There were problems sometimes, but nothing unsolvable. Costa remained there for the next three and a half years, until his death in November 2005.

While in the nursing home, Costa got the idea he wanted to buy a car. He even knew which car—a Lincoln. By this time he had been paralyzed for about four years. One of his current aides, Kuol, a fine and kindly fellow, said to Costa, "So you want to buy a car." By then, he had heard this dozens of times. "We will go outside to the van (the van I had bought early in Costa's illness and retrofitted for his use), and I will open the door for you. If you can get behind the wheel and drive, Momma will buy you a car." I was Momma and Costa was Daddo to Kuol.

Kuol opened the van door and Costa said, "Help me stand up. Help me into the van."

Kuol stood him up and Costa tried to move. Kuol was ready to support him of course, being strong and capable. Costa just stood there and finally said, "I can't."

"Well then, sit back down, Daddo. How can you drive a car when you can't get into it?"

This was how it went. Useless talk. Costa could never accept that his body was not in the condition to do what his mind wanted.

Though all three of the other children were at a distance from Grand Rapids, Stephanie and Katherine came with their children whenever possible. John did the same.

Penny returned to her physical therapy work. Three or four afternoons a week when she was finished at the hospital, she would pass by the nursing home to visit her father. If I was in town, I would also be waiting for her. We would have a glass of wine or tea, and share a bit of food together. Each day, Costa waited impatiently for Penny's arrival. It was the highlight of his day.

After the stroke, Costa never really improved, but gradually and slowly worsened. During the first year, he would read the newspapers a bit, watch some tennis or *Walker, Texas Ranger* on television. He had few visitors through the years. Most of his friends were scattered around the globe.

At times he was very unhappy—naturally. He had always been such a strong man, both mentally and physically. He continued asking to go with me to the Middle East—Cairo, Kuwait, or Beirut, anywhere. He wanted to "buy a car, buy a house, go to Cairo, go to Kuwait." On and on. It was impossible for him to understand that he could no longer do any of these things. This caused him great frustration and anger. It was only at the very end—if ever—he accepted his condition.

During the first year of the stroke, I sometimes would ask him questions about the businesses. Mostly he could not answer. Finally, he said, "I can't help you," or "I cannot remember." I stopped asking. This, however, did not stop him from wanting to go back to the Middle East. When I would try to explain why I could not take him, he often would become angry and belligerent.

Once when we were still in the house in Alexandria, Penny and I had invited a few good friends for cake and champagne. It was Costa's birthday. I had just returned from Cairo with a bad chest cold and of course was very tired. We all were enjoying our visit, when Costa burst out saying, "She ruined all my business in the Middle East. She ruined everything for me!"

Costa could not accept the fact that he would no longer return to the work that had been his life for so many years. The stroke had ruined him. Our friend, Craig Miller, who was close to both of us, came to Costa, put his arm around him, and said, "Costa, try to understand— Jessie is doing the best she can. Please don't be upset about any of this." Craig was able to calm him down, and we went on with the birthday celebration.

Liquidation

When we had come to New York for Bill Polk's birthday party in March of 1999, the plan was to stay for three days. Two weeks after Costa ended up in St. Luke's Roosevelt Hospital, I needed to return to our apartment in Washington to change clothes, check the mail, and begin figuring out what to do next. John drove me back and I spent two days at home.

I well knew there lay an enormous task ahead of me. A detailed plan, without which I could do *nothing*, was absolutely essential. My worry was that all of our businesses would be lost or stolen without Costa at the helm. These were my thoughts:

- *This must begin immediately. Not next week, nor next month, but* now.
- *Costa may be ill for a long time to come;*
- *He may never walk again; never be able to function properly;*
- *I must get some understanding of the businesses;*
- *I must find a way to liquidate in an orderly and gainful manner;*
- *Costa may* never *be well again!*

Though my husband was a brilliant man, in the latter years I believe he over-extended and expected too much of himself, which undoubtedly contributed to his downfall and illness. Years earlier, he understood that he needed to sell the house in Chios while he was alive and well, because I alone would never be able to manage the legal work. However, he made no such provisions with regard to his businesses. Instead of winding down his work, or contemplating what would happen if he could no longer function, he continued to expand, as though he would live forever.

Taking a spiral notebook, I began detailing one by one, the countries in which we were involved. At the same time, listing in each place, the lawyer and or friends—if any!—whom I would and could trust. Then, the partner, accountant, number one and/or associate employee in each country. I well knew, without a doubt, that in some instances there would be little or perhaps no cooperation at all, from some of them.

I began to prepare for the next of many trips to the Middle East with the sole purpose of liquidating all that Costa had built up over the years. This trip would be a fact-finding mission. First and foremost, my need was to learn what documents were necessary to be in hand to function, as well as to qualify me to take charge of the liquidation. I knew well that there was no way on this earth that I could manage and/or run these businesses on my own.

Because I knew that powers of attorney (PAs) from Costa were necessary before I could reach square one, this was where I began. These PAs would first need to be certified by the Department of State then further certified by the respective embassy of each country I must deal with. Of course, in some cases visas needed to be obtained. Fortunately, having lived in Washington, I well knew the locations of the various diplomatic missions. Lebanon was the least complicated. Because I was a bona fide partner of our Beirut company, J. Rudolph and Co., I could operate there without a power of attorney.

I went to work obtaining all PAs, certifications, visas and stamps, signed, sealed and delivered for the countries concerned.

Dubai

While in Cairo putting the necessary paperwork in place, I phoned John Cook in London to inform him of Costa's illness, my situation and some of my plans. I told him I wanted to go to Dubai. Both John and I knew that for more than a year Costa had wanted to exit this Dubai partnership. Since John was also a partner in the operation, I believed finalization could be quickly implemented. That was correct.

John and his wife Lexi had been our good friends for years, and I knew beyond the shadow of a doubt that I could trust John. I told him that I wanted Costa's complete withdrawal from the company in Dubai. He told me he would arrange the details for finalization and would call me back in a day or two. He did so. When I asked him to go to Dubai with me, he said, "I will meet you there. When do you want to go?"

We decided within ten days. Dubai is a six-hour flight from London, and John was there when I arrived. Within two days the matter was settled. John returned to London. I flew back to Cairo. If Costa could have chosen a younger brother, it would have been John Cook. He was a loyal friend with a great sense of humor.

The year prior to Costa's stroke, I had given a large dinner party to celebrate his 75th birthday in Washington D.C. and invited many of our friends, including John and Lexi, we'd known through the years. John and Lexi decided to surprise Costa. While clearing passport control, they were asked the purpose of their visit. "We've come for dinner," John told the official.

When we all first met, John had already been a few years in the employ of Carreras, the English cigarette company. Because Costa had made the arrangement for obtaining this agency for one of our companies, we became associated with John Cook. Soon he and Lexi visited us in Beirut, and our deep friendship began. After a number of meetings in the '60s—perhaps six or eight—I asked John, "Don't you have a different tie?" I had no idea of the significance of the same tie he wore *all* the time.

"This is my school tie from Sandhurst. I always wear it." Undoubtedly this tie had been replaced a number of times over the years. John not only was an ex-British Army officer, he was a graduate of the prestigious Sandhurst.

"Well, when are you going to get a different tie?" I asked.

"I haven't gotten around to it yet."

Finally I bought his first new tie that was *not* a Sandhurst tie. To this day, we can still smile about this.

Kuwait

Kuwait had a history. This was because the first office which Costa opened in the Gulf—the Arabian Gulf—was in Kuwait in 1960. In many respects Kuwait was a base for Costa. Then, too, we did live there in the late 1970s, some of the worst war years in Lebanon. So when I shipped Samsonite from Port Said to Kuwait, I felt reasonably sure the merchandise would be sold at a profit and credited to the office. I did the same with a large Sheaffer shipment—again shipped from Port Said to Kuwait. The decisions I made, no doubt, were not the ones that Costa would have chosen, but I did what I *needed* to do, and without delay.

When Costa became ill, we were deep into a court case with the Sheaffer Pen Company for a few hundred thousand dollars. I made five or six trips to Kuwait, meeting there with Zuhair, our lawyer. Also there were numerous phone calls between us, usually initiated by me. Each time I was told that the case was progressing well, and soon we would be collecting from Sheaffer. Zuhair needed to be paid for his efforts. The last and final payment he asked for was $10,000. I transferred the money to him from Beirut, but he did not acknowledge my transfer. After three weeks, I phoned him. He said he had received the money. I asked that he keep me informed about the Sheaffer court case; he never contacted me again. I dropped the matter entirely, not wanting to throw any more good money after bad.

Costa probably would not have approved, but I had been prodding and pestering this lawyer for more than two years. Simply speaking, I gave up. I have always believed that if anything did come our way from Sheaffer, Zuhair, who had originally been given full power of attorney from Costa to collect from Sheaffer, was the winner; I, the loser. God only knows what really happened here, but no doubt Zuhair was expecting me to give up. He was right. I did.

Egypt

Only after liquidating the Dubai, Kuwait and Saudi Arabia businesses, did I concentrate on Egypt. It took more than two years to finalize and salvage as much as possible from Cairo and Port Said. I knew this would be a long and slow process and was expecting these two locations would be my greatest challenges, and perhaps my greatest losses. They were.

When in Cairo, I had already made numerous trips to Port Said, which is a two and a half hour car trip across the desert—east to Ismalia, the Suez Canal, then north to Port Said.

A bit of background: Port Said is located on the Mediterranean at the mouth of the Suez Canal. The city is a Free Zone. The north and south ports of the of the Canal are extremely busy, both in Port Said and Suez, with ships busily plying the Canal. During the mornings, ships sail south; in the afternoons, ships sail north. Unlike the Panama Canal, the Suez Canal is no more than 200 to 250 yards wide at any one given point and cannot accommodate two ships passing side by side. Recently I have read that the Canal is being widened, but only in a certain area.

Because Port Said funnels the heavier traffic through to Suez, it is only natural that there be duty-free facilities within the transit area. Costa recognized and was well aware of all this. He intended to take advantage of these duty-free possibilities. In the 1970s, he opened an office, rented an apartment, and bought two warehouses in the Duty Free Zone.

Early on, I had been given names of consultants, supposedly experts at liquidating and wrapping up businesses—anywhere! With the exception of one man in Port Said, I never pursued any of them. I refer to Farouk Fattah. He, in particular, was knowledgeable, knew all the authorities in town, and he had known Costa at another time. Like most Egyptians, Farouk could be trusted only to a certain extent. He was instrumental in the sale of the larger of the two warehouses. All did not turn out rosy, but it worked. For a while anyway. After about three months I realized there needed to be a parting of ways between Farouk and myself. I paid him for his efforts and bade him goodbye.

At one point, our son John had taken leave from his work at Harvard and came to Cairo to help and support me. He remained about two months. This visit didn't turn out well. Even though John knew and understood these people, he could not tolerate any of them. One particular day at the Cairo office, he and one of the employees argued, then began to physically fight each other. The other person was smaller than John. I did manage to separate them because I was frightened someone would call the police, and John would be taken to jail. If that had happened, only God could help me! After this incident, John never returned to Egypt.

After a couple of weeks, and still aware that I needed a person known to me and whom I could trust to be my eyes and ears in Port Said, I phoned John in Boston and asked him about his friend Hassan Zobi, a Lebanese. He was an ex-Kuwait employee of ours who still lived in Kuwait. I told John what I had in mind, which was to bring Hassan to Port Said to help me out, to keep him there—all expenses paid—for the next few months. John gave me his blessing. I phoned Hassan in Kuwait, and within the week he had arrived in Egypt; he remained there for the next three months for me. Hassan was by no means perfect; however, he was better than what was in Port Said. Besides, he listened to me.

Both of the warehouses which Costa had purchased in the Free Zone in the 1980s had remained totally empty all those years. He had had the idea to do assembly there. What assembly, I no longer remember, or perhaps never knew. The larger warehouse was now sold, and I badly needed to sell, and be rid of the smaller one. The process was tedious and time-consuming, but with the help of Hassan, within the next three months we had finalized the sale of the second warehouse. We had been satisfactorily compensated, and there was a certain degree of satisfaction.

Not all transactions turned out this well. The Cairo office was especially problematic. As an example, we had a shipment of Beck's Beer, German origin, one of our agencies, arriving from Hamburg. I knew it was coming through Port Said. Merchandise either arrived through Alexandria or Port Said then was transshipped to Cairo. It was near-beer or 1% alcohol, and the only beer allowed to be imported and sold on the Egyptian open market. The consignment had been personally paid for by Costa before he became ill. The amount—$50,000. As I had for some time known of this expected beer consignment, for a number of weeks I continued to ask our Egyptian partner, Shukri, now in charge of the office, "Where is the beer shipment? When will it arrive?"

"It's coming."

"It's on the way."

"It's coming soon."

Sometime later, perhaps six or eight weeks, and after asking again and again, Shukri told me, "Oh, it's finished."

"What do you mean, finished?"

"It's been sold," he answered.

"Where's the money?" I asked.

"It's finished."

Again, "What do you mean, finished?"

All he would say was, "It's finished."

I was all but trembling with anger, but could say no more. Previously, when learning that Costa had personally paid for the consignment, and now knowing that the office had stolen the lot of it, I knew well, I had no power in Egypt. If done properly, our merchandise would have arrived in Port Said or Alexandria, and transshipped to our warehouse in Cairo, then distributed to the locations where pre-sales were often made.

All Shukri would tell me was, "It's finished." Undoubtedly it was.

Our attorney, Yassin Tageddin, confirmed with me that there was nothing to be done about the beer shipment.

The beer was not the only issue. Our in-town warehouse had been stocked with thousands of dollars' worth of Samsonite luggage as well as Sheaffer pens, along with various other items. When I asked to go visit the warehouse, again with a big grin, I was told, "It's finished." When told this, I decided this was to be the end of Cairo operations.

Fortunately, the Cairo office held no control over the Port Said business, so when we had a large shipment of Samsonite arrive in Port Said, I got busy. Knowing that most –maybe all—would be lost or stolen, I phoned our Kuwait office and told them, "I have $150,000 of Samsonite sitting in customs here. If I don't get it out immediately, it will be confiscated or stolen. We will lose it." Within three days it was on its way to our Kuwait office.

When I told the international representative of Samsonite, Hadi Farah, what I had done, he said, "You can't do that!"

My answer was, "Hadi, I have done it. Had it remained here, it would have been stolen too."

Hadi said no more because his dislike for the Egyptians was intense.

Cairo

Our French-educated attorney Yassin Tageddin carried a well-respected presence in Egypt. He was a great asset to me in my time of need. He knew well my feelings and opinions of most, if not all of our employees. He also knew Costa well and had a very good understanding of our Egyptian businesses. I retained Yassin throughout the Egyptian liquidations. I always believed he fully supported my thinking even though my son John did not agree with me on this.

The apartment in which I was living, (where Costa and I had moved to when we lost our villa) though near enough to the Cairo office, was not where I wanted to be. I wanted to return to Zamalek, where we had previously lived and where most of our friends lived. I wanted and needed to be closer to our dear friends, Joe and Ellie Sheridan. Also Yassin's office was located not far away in Mohandessin. So, I found an apartment that was furnished with (what once had been beautiful) old and dirty furniture and moved back to Zamalek. By this time, I had released Mohamed the cook as well as Noura, the Eritrean maid, but retained Souad, the Egyptian maid who was quite a good cook, and the houseboy, Young Mohamed, who doubled as a driver. Our old driver, Mahmoud, had died shortly after Costa became ill.

Zamalek is an island in the Nile River. Just north of Cairo, the Nile separates, and the area in the midst, perhaps eight to ten miles in length and a mile or so wide, is Zamalek. This island is densely populated and reputed to enjoy cooler temperatures than the other areas of Cairo during the summer months. Many expatriates reside there, i.e. most of the foreign community.

My apartment was located within walking distance of the Sheridans. When I visited them, sometimes in the evenings, Souad would walk with me there. When the visit was over, we phoned her and she would come to walk home with me.

When I needed to visit the lawyer, Yassin, it would be in the evenings, 8:00 p.m. and sometimes later. Young Mohamed would drive me there, wait for me in the outside office, sometimes until 10:00 p.m. or more, then drive me back to the apartment. As I trusted no one in the Cairo office, I went nowhere alone.

Costa and I had accumulated stacks of boxes overflowing with documents and papers, primarily regarding the airport duty-free business and CAA problems. One evening I told Yassin I did not know what to do with all these files and documents, as long as nothing would ever be resolved in our favor, and I intended to give up Egypt. The following week Yassin spent a day with me in my apartment, sorting through box after box. What we didn't throw away, he took and put into storage. Where, I never knew. As Shukri would say, "It is finished."

Lebanon

Closing the Beirut office was the least of my problems, and I left it until the very end of my quest. In the early 2000s, J. Rudolph & Co was making money, the employees were doing their jobs, and I had no complaints. Besides, I enjoyed my trips there, spending time daily in the office. There were no real problems, and I was content to leave well enough alone until mid-2006, after Costa's death. It was then that I decided to hand over the Samsonite agency, the final and only company we represented, to the Halim Hanna group.

We closed J. Rudolph and Co.'s office once and for all. Of the seven employees, four were discharged. The remaining three went along with the Samsonite agency to become part of the Hanna Group.

Dimitri Hanna, his brother Richard, and young Halim, son of Dimitri, were happy to acquire Samsonite. They still hold the agency and continue to do very well with it.

I, too, have been happy that the Hannas took the Samsonite agency, an agency that our companies had held since 1966. Our friendship with this family goes back for more than 50 years. On my Beirut trips it is my great pleasure to spend time at their office to visit with this family, as well as some of our old employees.

Costa's Final Journey

There was a Door to which I found no Key:
There was a Veil past which I could not see;
Some little Talk awhile of Me and Thee
There seemed—and then no more of Thee and Me.

Omar Khayám, *The Rubáiyát*

After his hemorrhagic stroke on March 6, 1999, Costa lived six years and eight months. The last three months of his life found him in a much deteriorated condition; he spoke little and hardly answered any questions. It was as though he was gradually melting away. By mid-October 2005, he was eating less and less. Both Penny and I would try to please and tempt him with dishes we knew he had always loved. Even in these, he showed little or no interest. The last two weeks of his life, he stopped eating altogether. The final and last two or three days, he took no water. We knew the end was near.

Both Penny and Terry sat with me, near Costa throughout the night before he died. He seemed to go to sleep. At a few minutes before seven a.m. on Monday, November 7, 2005, he died peacefully. Immediately I phoned Stephanie and Katherine to let them know their father had passed away. John did not answer his phone, so after a number of trials, I left the news on his answering machine.

As I had already made funeral arrangements, the funeral home was notified immediately. They came and took him away. By early evening Costa's body was prepared. Penny, Terry, the aides Kuol and William, and I went to visit. I was pleased. Early morning, Tuesday, the following day, Costa's last and final journey began. Late afternoon he arrived at the funeral home in Wickliffe, Kentucky where prior arrangements had been made for visitation.

By Tuesday noon, Penny, Stephanie and Katherine, Randy and Terry, as well as the eight grandchildren had arrived. I was waiting for them. In the afternoon John arrived in Kentucky. He had returned the night before from Cannes in France. Now all the family had assembled. Surely, Costa was looking down from heaven and saying, "Well, finally they are all together, here, for me."

Visitation was announced in the local newspaper the day before, and a number of old friends were in attendance. All the children and grandchildren had arrived. Costa's funeral was held at 10:00 a.m. on Wednesday, November 9th, at Bethlehem Baptist Church.

The eight grandchildren were all nicely dressed: the boys in blue blazers and gray pants and the girls in pretty dresses and patent leather shoes. Pallbearers were John Halkias, Terry Haines, Randy Dalia, Chuckie Dennis, Jimmy Holt, and Kuol Anyang.

Costa's casket was draped with the American flag, and a trumpeter was present to sound *Taps*. Three Waves were also present. They removed the flag from the casket, folded it, and presented it to me.

Each of the grandchildren had been given a red rose. Once the vault with casket had been lowered, each child dropped his/her rose along with a handful of dirt into the grave.

After the burial, lunch was served in the hospitality room of the church. That evening we, the entire family, went for dinner together. The following day, all of us left for home.

Thus, after 54 years, the major chapter of my life ended.

Epilogue

The Moving Finger writes; and having writ,
Moves on: nor all the Piety nor Wit
Shall lure it back to cancel half a Line,
Nor all the Tears wash out a word of it.

Omar Khayám, *The Rubáiyát*

Katherine, Stephanie, me, and Penny, 2014

The year after Costa passed away, his younger sister Thalia went into a deep depression. I never really knew the full story; however, she turned to our children, John and Katherine, for help. Although far away, they both were willing to do their best to help her. Thalia had always depended upon Costa; now that he was gone, she became lost. She phoned for John and Katherine and asked them to come to Athens. They spent a week with her. The following year, in March, they were called back. A cousin had committed her to a mental hospital, and she was trying her best to get away from the hospital. It is costly to get on a plane in Boston and fly to Athens, and besides both of them were working. Nevertheless, John and Katherine went again and spent a week or so with her.

Thalia convinced John and Katherine to get her released from the mental hospital. She didn't want them to leave and even wanted John to become a co-signer on her bank account. He did not wish to become involved in her affairs from such a distance and refused her. Within a few days they returned to Boston.

After Katherine and John left Athens, she continued to call them often. However, in May, a neighbor Ioanna (no relative) phoned John to tell him that Thalia was dead. She had thrown herself from her balcony of the fourth floor of the building and was found the following morning. She had given up. John and Katherine again returned to Athens to take charge of her burial.

Over the years, I remained friends with Mrs. Curdie's son Justin from the boarding house at 906 Grant Street, and his wife Isabelle. Whenever Costa and I visited the Samsonite offices in Denver, we would meet for dinner with Justin and Isabelle. In turn, they visited us in Boston, North Conway, Indianapolis, Kentucky and New York.

Isabelle had died sometime before Costa's stroke. When I was moving from Washington/Alexandria to Michigan, Justin came to visit a few times and we spoke often on the phone. He had good relationships with my children, for which I was most grateful.

A year after Costa passed away, Justin, who still lived in Denver, encouraged me to move there. Shortly after purchasing an apartment and arriving in Denver, I learned that he had fallen for a woman whom he planned to marry. This news made no sense to me, but what does one do?

I moved on and took up playing bridge again with various friends at our homes and the University Club where I had become an active member. I've continued to travel to the Middle East as well as other places which interest me.

Sometime passed after Justin's marriage ended—a disaster which left him nearly penniless—and he contacted me again. We met for lunch at Rodney's, one of our old hang outs in the Cherry Creek area. I was shocked when he showed up in ragged jeans and a ponytail.

It turned out Justin was quite humbled by his experience. I decided we could be friends again if he would dress respectably and behave himself. Definitely, the ponytail had to go. We resumed our friendship, but I never again trusted him. Eventually I offered to rent him a small apartment which I had recently bought, but let him know the rent *must* be paid on time! It was. Also I bought a small car for him to use, putting the title in both our names. We had a contract: once a month he made a car payment to me towards the car, and when he died, the car was mine. We remained friends until his death on November 5, 2011.

Even after the office in Beirut was closed, I have continued traveling there to visit with old friends. In January, 2011, Penny and John joined me for a visit. They arrived on a Saturday, and we spent a lovely Sunday together. That morning, we visited the grave site of Penny's son, Stephen, and enjoyed a coffee outing. The wife of Jacob, Costa's cousin, had died the day before so that evening we went to pay our respects.

We left Jacob's house to walk to the restaurant for dinner, a three-block walk. I was walking ahead of John and Penny when I noticed there was a motor bike going the wrong way on a one-way street. I thought, *they must be lost*, and turned to see what was going on. There were two men on the bike. They grabbed my handbag and one of them slammed me hard. I fell backwards to the street. A man driving by immediately saw what had happened. He wheeled around and shouted at Penny and John, "Get her in the car," which they did. He drove us to the American University Hospital which was very near. I ended up spending six days there with a concussion. The nausea along with a headache was something I'd never experienced in my life. Penny stayed with me day and night; John came every day, but spent the nights at his hotel. They both agonized over me, and John truly believed I was going to die.

The police came to the hospital and filed a report, but nothing came of it. The robbers had taken about $600 in cash, all my credit cards, along with my favorite wallet. The Consul from the American Embassy also came to the hospital to visit. I never understood why the Consul or the police bothered. Luckily, just before we went to pay our respects to Jacob, I had decided to leave my passport in the hotel room, so that was not an issue.

After a few days, John could bear it no longer. On Friday, he told me, "I'm leaving, and I'll never come back here again." He didn't.

Lots of friends came to visit, as well as our dear friend, Father Donahue. The medical staff was excellent. My doctor was the eldest son of some of my dearest Beirut friends. George is one of the foremost, if not the foremost, neurosurgeons in the Middle East. I believe I would never have received such attention at a hospital anywhere else in the world. The greatest annoyance was John, Penny, and I were so looking forward to a pleasant visit together, and our time was ruined—never to come back.

After six days, I was discharged. Penny stayed on another week and took great care of me. Her flight was scheduled to leave 4-5 days before my planned departure. She offered to change her flight so she could accompany me back to the States, but I said, "No, I'll be fine," and I was. When it was time to leave, I arranged to have a wheel chair take me around the airport which was not ideal. I did not like being on someone else's schedule.

Robbing people from a motor bike is fairly common practice in Beirut. The following year, a friend, the mother of George, the neurosurgeon, was standing on the curb waiting for her husband to come around with the car when men on a motor bike came along and tried to grab her handbag. They didn't succeed, but they threw her into the street and broke her pelvis bone. That's how her husband found her when he arrived with the car.

I still love to visit Beirut, but I am more careful now. I no longer walk alone in the evening, only during the day. At night, my friends and I take taxis for outings.

In November 2012, we were devastated, this time by the loss of John. This picture taken of him with his sister Katherine is how I like to remember him best—when he was happy with the world. Once when we were all together as a family, gathered at the lunch table, from out of

the blue, John said to Katherine, "Kashern, you are a piece of work."
He was five years old at the time.

John and Katherine, Falmouth, circa 1983

John had struggled to find his way in the world. He never could reconcile himself to work with his father in the Middle East, but he did remain in a job at Harvard for more than 20 years. Oh, how he loved Harvard! A nasty situation occurred, to which John was a victim and he lost his job in 2009. He was 46 years old and could not adjust to his plight. He never fully recovered.

About a year and a half after the Harvard incident, I talked John into going back to school. He enrolled at Bentley University in Waltham, Massachusetts. After a period of time, he began to enjoy Bentley and was happy again, but not entirely. John joined an exercise program at MIT where he played squash. He was a devoted and fine squash player and always prided himself in his game achievements. He was truly excellent. He quit playing the fall he died, just quit. We spoke daily on the phone when I was in the States, sometimes more than once, but I could understand that he had gained weight, and he wasn't feeling well.

Normally, when I was out of the country, we didn't speak on the phone. Phone calls are expensive, and I told the children to save their money. In 2012, just before Thanksgiving while I was in Beirut, John phoned me—unusual as it was, I was delighted to speak with him, and he was in fine spirits.

Two weeks later when I returned to Denver, I tried phoning him numerous times for two days, but no answer. I phoned Katherine and told her she must go immediately to John's house to see about him and find out why he was not answering his phone.

The front door was locked; John did not answer the door. Katherine brought in the police and fire department. They broke down the door to his town house. John was found kneeling next to the couch in the living room. He was dead.

John's death has been a devastating loss for me, as well as for his sisters. A funeral mass was held for him at St. Ignatius Church at Boston College. Many of John's friends attended, as well as friends of mine and the girls. Harvard was well represented; this would have pleased John immensely. I, too, was proud and sad.

The following day, John was then taken by air to the funeral home in Wickliffe, Kentucky, and from there onto Bethlehem Cemetery where my parents and Costa are buried. On December 1, 2012, after a short graveside service, we buried him next to his father.

It took three months to receive the results of the autopsy. The conclusion was his heart gave out—just quit. Losing John was not only devastating to me, it has left me feeling cheated, disappointed, angry and bitter. It has been my greatest disappointment and the sorrow of my life.

Yet my life continues. Rose Kennedy said it best when she spoke these words:

> It has been said, "Time heals all wounds." I do not agree. The wounds remain. In time, the mind, protecting the sanity, covers them with scar tissue and the pain lessens, but it is never gone.

Every fall I make a pilgrimage to Kentucky to visit the graves of my loved ones, and I continue to travel to Beirut twice or more a year, to reconnect with old friends. Last year, I sold my Cherry Creek home and moved into a rented apartment to give me time to plan the next stage of my life.

I have covered many, many miles and traveled a long way from the young girl lying in the Kentucky grass, dreaming about Mesopotamia. When this book is finished, I intend to keep traveling to new and familiar places, visiting old friends, making new ones, and spending time with my family for as long as this earthly body will allow me to do so. In the time left to me, I will continue as I have always done—living life my way.

On that note, I will let Will Rogers have the last word. In my case I hope he is wrong! He said, "There ain't nothing that breaks up homes, country and nations like somebody publishing memoirs."

Rudolph Family Tree

Fredrick Rudolph, born in 1738, of German origin came from Austria by way of Holland and Italy, where he married an Italian woman before emigrating to America in about 1760. He fathered one son and five daughters which all reached adult age. Abraham Rudolph III, the only son was born in 1764, and he fathered five sons. Many of the Rudolphs in the Carolinas, Virginias, Ohio, Kentucky, Tennessee, and other middle states are descended from Abraham Rudolph III. Jesse Thomas Rudolph was his great-great grandson.

On the Sherron side, the ancestors can be traced back to Joseph Shearin who was born in 1687. This side of the family had a soldier in the Revolutionary war and some of them owned slaves before the Civil war.

Jesse Thomas Ruldoph (see below) married his first cousin, Sarah E. Sherron. Jesse's mother, Elizabeth T. (Sherron) Rudolph, was sister to Sarah's father, Jesse Colman (Cole) Sherron. "Said to be a very large man, Jesse Coleman Sherron was apparently a colorful, personable and aggressive individual and leaves a long line of descendants most of whom use the Sherron spelling of the name."[9]

---

[9] Twelve generations of the SHERRONS can be found in *Descendants of Joseph SHEARIN 2* a family tree published by Charles Thomas Cantrell, a direct descendent of Joseph SHEARIN at http://www.familyorigins.com/users/c/a/n/Charles-T-Cantrell/FAMO1-0001/d911.html This website traces our branch of the SHERRON family down through Jesse Coleman SHERRON and Elizabeth T. SHERRON (sixth generation down from Joseph SHEARIN born in 1687) includes wills bequeathing slaves and Joseph SHEARIN (third generation) who died in the Revolutionary War. The SHERRON name was spelled many different ways including SHEARIN, SHERON, SHERRIN and SHERRON.

1.Jesse Thomas (Tom) RUDOLPH b. 13 Aug 1866, d. 20 June 1937

+ Sarah Elizabeth (Sallie) SHERRON b. 22 Mar 1871, d. Jan 1936

    2.Arley Allen RUDOLPH b. 17 Sept 1892, d. 27 Nov 1940 (stroke)

    +Thelma Trice (died of tuberculosis)

    + Girlene HOLT b. 19 Feb 1908, m. 30 Dec 1926, d. 20 March 1990 (cancer)

        3.Morris A. RUDOLPH b. May 1928, d. June 2011

        +Florence QUICK b. Nov 1928, m. 16 Oct 1949, d. July 2012

            4.Marcus Edwin RUDOLPH b. 16 Feb 1955

            4.David Norman RUDOLPH b. Nov 1961

                5.Jeremiah David b. 1980

                    6.two sons

                5.Joshua RUDOLPH

                    6.three sons

                5.Justin RUDOLPH

      3.Jessie Arlene RUDOLPH b. 30 May 1929, m. 25 Oct 1951 in Beirut
and again 16 Jan 1952 in Baghdad

      +Constantine John (Costa) Halkias b. 26 Feb 1923, d. 7 Nov 2005

          4.John Constantine HALKIAS b. 2 Aug. 1952 in West
Suburban Hospital, Chicago, IL, d. 18 Nov 1952,
(crib death in Baghdad)

          4.Penelope Anne Therese HALKIAS b. 3 October 1953 in
Dar es Salam Hospital, Baghdad, m. 25 July 1975

          +Thomas William HICKS b. May 1952

              5.Brian Anthony HICKS b. 29 Nov 1978 (Peoria),
m. 20 Dec 2003

              +Marissa KUHN

                  6.Sophie HICKS b. 20 Sept 2009

              5.Stephen James HICKS b. 4 Nov 1980, d. 12 Nov 1980
in Jeddah. (buried in Beirut 25 Nov, 1980)

          +Terence HAINES m. 1995

4.Stephanie Christine HALKIAS b. 18 July 1957 in Haideri
Hospital, Baghdad, m. 16 Oct 1982

+ Randall John (Randy) DALIA b. Dec 1957

> **5.Christopher John DALIA** b. 17 April 1989

> **5.Sarah Elizabeth DALIA** b. 1 Dec 1990

> **5.Erin Christine DALIA** b. 19 Oct 1993

> **5. Katherine Anne DALIA** b. 8 Aug 1996

4.Katherine Constantine HALKIAS b. 26 Sept 1961 in Khaldy
Hospital, Beirut, m. 30 April 1988

+David BOEGEHOLD

> **5.Benjamin David BOEGEHOLD** b. 15 Feb 1990

> **5.Samuel David BOEGEHOLD** b. 23 April 1992

> **5.Lukas David BOEGEHOLD** b. 26 Feb 1996

+Robert B. GRAHAM m. 23 August 2008

4.Constantine John HALKIAS, II b. 5 Nov 1963 in Khaldy
Hospital, Beirut, adopted Nov 1963, d. 30 Nov 2012

2.Elvin Davis (Uncle Davis) RUDOLPH (disabled) b. 1902, d. 5 Nov 1939.

2.Female RUDOLPH (died at birth)

Holt Family Tree

Mother's side of the family

Minnie Lee Reeves, wife of Norman Edward Holt was Irish and Native American. Her grandmother, a member of the Chickasaw tribe, married into the Reeves family who were Irish descendants. Many of Girlene's sayings came from the Irish.

My brother, Morris worked on our genealogy for a number of years. The work he did was, I believe, inaccurate, full of tall tales and is not included here.

1.**Norman Edward HOLT** b. 5 Jan 1880, m. 27 Jan 1902 (farmer), d. June 1971

+ **Minnie Lee REEVES** b. 24 Dec 1881, d. 4 Oct. 1964 (daughter of George REEVES and

Betty BRINNEY of Ballard Cty, KY)

    2.Edmond Lee HOLT b. 27 May 1904, d. 27 Nov 1904

    2.J.L. (Jack) HOLT b. 21 Jan 1906

    +Jeanette

        3.Jessie HOLT

            4. three children

        3.Rosemary HOLT

            4. four children

        3.Gary HOLT

            4. two adopted children

    + Louise

        3.Minnie Sue HOLT

    2.**Girlene HOLT** b. 19 Feb, 1908, m. 30 Dec 1926, d. 10 March 1990 (cancer)

    + **Arley A. RUDOLPH** b. 17 Sept 1892, d. 27 Nov 1940 (stroke)

        [See 3rd generation of the RUDOLPH family]

+David S. Longnecker 30 May 1942 (no children)

2.Ollie James HOLT b. 2 Oct 1911, m. 5 Jan 1934, d. 12 Jan 2001

+Viola CARPENTER

2.James Edward (Jimmy) HOLT b. 5 Dec 1943 (adopted), m.31 May 1965

+ Diann POLOVICK

       3.James (Jamie) HOLT b. 12 Jan 1968

       3.Julianna (Julie) HOLT

2.Elton Bert HOLT b. 12 June 1914, d. 10 June 1946

+Lucille CARPENTER

       3.Billy Bert HOLT b. 17 April 1943, m. 20 Oct 1967

Halkias Family Tree

(originally Halkiyas)

John George Halkias was born about 1811, at Kardamyla, Chios. His family fled to the Island of Psara, then to the Peloponnesus during the Greek Revolution of 1822. He was one of four brothers whose father's name was George Halkias. Later John George returned to Chios with his parents and brothers, Stamatis, Constantinos and Theodore. This was one of the oldest and best known families in Kardamyla. Around 1840, John George married Irene Frances who was also from Kardamyla. Irene's mother was from the Phokas family and always related to Irene and her four brothers that she came from a distinguished family in Constantinople. "I am a Phokas" she always told everyone. The nephew of Emperor Nikephoros Phokas, Bardas Phokas had been sent to exile in Chios by his cousin, the Emperor John I Tzimiskes, and Irene was a descendant from this branch of the Phokas family.

The information about the Halkias family came from Uncle Mike. One afternoon, he sat down and told me everything he could about the Halkias family.

1.John George HALKIAS b. 1811, m. 1840, d. 1887

+Irene Frances

    2.George HALKIAS b. 1842, d. 1875

    2.Michael HALKIAS b. 1845, d. 1878

    2.Demosthenes

        3.John

        3.Katherine

    2.Theodora HALKIAS b. 1847, d. 1872

    +Dimitri KALMOUKAS

3.Dimitri

3.Theodore

3.Aristidis

2.Nicolas HALKIAS b. 1849, d. 1880 (a monk)

2.Pandelis HALKIAS b. 1852, d. 1872

2.Theodoros HALKIAS b. 1854, d. 1872

2.Constantine John HALKIAS b. 1861, d. 1937

+Marigho NEAMONITIS (YiaYiá) (daughter of Nicholas Neomontis and

Perdhika Palanide) b. 1869 d. 1964

    3.Theodora HALKIAS b. 1888, d. 1925

    + Nicholas SIRMAKIDIS

        4.Ioanna SIRMAKIDIS b. 1915, d. 1925

    3.John Constantine HALKIAS b. 1891, d. 1948

    +Eugenie Minassian b 1901 (Izmir, Turkey), d. 1980

        4.Constantine John HALKIAS b. 26 Feb 1923 in Baghdad,

        m. 25 Oct1951, d. 7 Nov 2005

        +Jessie Arlene RUDOLPH

            5.[see third generation of RUDOLPH family]

        4.Maria John HALKIAS b.1924, d. 1996

        +Vassily SPIROPOULOUS

            5.Marigho (Margie) SPIROPOULOUS b. 1954,

                6. one son

            5.Anastasis Vassily SPIROPOULOUS b. March 1957,

            d. 1998

            5.female SPIROPOULOUS, died at approximate age

            of two

        4.Thalia John HALKIAS b. April 1929, d. 2006

        (divorced, no children)

3.Nicholas Constantine (Nico) HALKIAS b. 1893, d. 1944

+Irene LIRAS

    4.GeorgeNicholas HALKIAS b. 1932

    4.ElizabethNicholas HALKIAS b. 1934

    4.ConstantineNicholas HALKIAS b. 1943

3.Irene HALKIAS b. 1896, d. 1980

+Sacrates MOSCHOVIS

    4.John Sacrates MOSCHOVIS b. 1924

3.George Constantine HALKIAS b. 1899

+Anastasia POLITI d. 1943 (insane)

    4.Constantine George HALKIAS b. 1930

    4.Panayotes George HALKIAS b. 1932

+Katina POLAVIDES

    4.Stella HALKIAS b. 1949

3.Michael (Uncle Mike) Constantine HALKIAS b. 1900, d. 1971

3.Demosthenes (Uncle Demo) Constantine HALKIAS b. 1902, d.˜1993

+Angelike (Kiki) d.˜1982

    4.Constantine D. HALKIAS b. 1965

    4.Vassily D. HALKIAS b. 1969, d. 1988

3.Marianthe HALKIAS b. 1905, d. 1992

+Apostolos STAVRINAKI

    4.Katherine (Katia) STAVRINAKI b. 1941

    + Dimitri POULOUDIS

        5.Anastasia POULOUDIS

        5.Maria POULOUDIS

22237024R00167

Made in the USA
San Bernardino, CA
26 June 2015